12.00

ALLERTON PARK INSTITUTE

Number 24

Papers Presented at the Allerton Park Institute

Sponsored by

University of Illinois
Graduate School of Library Science

held

November 12-15, 1978
Allerton House
Monticello, Illinois

Supervision of Employees in Libraries

ROLLAND E. STEVENS

Editor

University of Illinois
Graduate School of Library Science
Urbana-Champaign, Illinois

Library of Congress Cataloging in Publication Data

Allerton Park Institute, 24th, 1978.
    Supervision of employees in libraries.

    "Papers presented at the Allerton Park Institute,
sponsored by University of Illinois Graduate School
of Library Science, held November 12-15, 1978,
Allerton House, Monticello, Illinois."
    1. Library personnel management — Congresses.
I. Stevens, Rolland Elwell, 1915- II. Illinois. University at
Urbana-Champaign. Graduate School of Library
Science.
Z682.A38   1978   658.3′7′02   79-10860
ISBN 0-87845-051-3

CONTENTS

Introduction

On November 12-15, 1978, the University of Illinois Graduate School of Library Science sponsored its twenty-fourth annual Allerton Park Institute at Allerton House, located about twenty-five miles southwest of Champaign. The theme chosen by the faculty of the Graduate School of Library Science for this year's institute was "Supervision of Employees in Libraries." A planning committee was appointed of the following faculty and library staff: Margaret Chaplan, Librarian, Institute of Labor and Industrial Relations; Thomas Gaughan, Director of Library Personnel; Maurine Pastine, Librarian, Undergraduate Library; Rolland Stevens, Professor, Graduate School of Library Science; and Herbert Goldhor, Director, Graduate School of Library Science. These people compiled a list of topics and activities to be included in the 4-day institute, as well as names of persons to be invited to present papers. Herbert Goldhor wrote to prospective speakers; made necessary arrangements with the help of the Allerton House staff, and Edward Kalb and Donald Campbell (of the university's Office of Continuing Education and Public Service); prepared news releases about the forthcoming institute; previewed and selected an appropriate training film to be used in the program; and handled many other details. Since he was on sabbatical leave during fall 1978 and unable to participate in the November institute, I conducted the sessions in his absence and edited the papers for publication.

The institute was planned for persons who are now (or soon expect to be) first-line supervisors in libraries in order to provide them with practical assistance in learning how to perform their supervisory responsibilities. All types of libraries were to be covered, with emphasis on public and academic libraries of medium to large size, as these are the libraries in which problems of supervision arise most often and in which principles of good supervision have, therefore, the most useful application. Supervision of both clerical and professional library employees was covered in the program.

Those persons who attended and participated in the institute derived much benefit that is not available to those who read these proceedings but were not present at the meetings: the sharing of meals and living quarters; the exchange of ideas in the question-and-answer period of each meeting, in the halls and at the table; and the stimulation of meeting and communicating with the speakers. These various advantages were rated above the papers themselves by the participants. Still, we hope that these published papers will be of benefit to those who were not able to be at Allerton House.

The institute opened with a self-graded test of leadership potential, which was explained, administered and analyzed by Richard A. Mannweiler, Professor of the Institute of Labor and Industrial Relations at the University of Illinois. The objective of his analysis was to explain the interrelationship of task-oriented and relationship-oriented styles of leadership and to examine typical situations in which one or the other of these styles is more appropriate. Because the test itself is of little value without Mannweiler's analysis, it is not reproduced here. The first papers presented in the program were a keynote address and several reviews of the theory and research of supervision. Later papers tended more toward aspects of application and practical advice to the supervisor.

Another valuable part of the institute which unfortunately could not become part of the published proceedings was the practice session of supervisor/employee role-playing, conducted by Geraldine King. Following her short demonstration of appropriate verbal and nonverbal behavior in a confrontation between supervisor and employee, members of the audience divided into groups of three, alternating as supervisor, employee and observer. Those who participated felt that they learned more about how to handle situations of this kind by practicing than they could have by hearing a paper.

One of the most well received sessions of the conference was the discussion by a panel of five relatively new supervisors who each described some of their initial problems and what they did to solve them. Since these presentations did not result in an actual paper, they have been summarized here under the title "Making the Transition from Employee to Supervisor," prepared by Holly Wagner, Technical Editor of the Graduate School of Library Science.

Thanks are due the members of the planning committee for their suggestions of topics and speakers for the conference and for chairing sessions. Members of the Graduate School of Library Science faculty and staff, and staff members of the university's Office of Continuing Education and Public Service, also assisted in the meetings and in the lengthy preparations for the institute. Lastly, the work of the Publications Office in preparing these papers for publication is gratefully acknowledged.

ROLLAND E. STEVENS
Editor

HUGH C. ATKINSON
Director
University of Illinois Library
Urbana-Champaign

The Importance of Good Supervision in Libraries

The importance of good supervision is obvious, so this paper will concentrate instead on the meaning of good supervision and some of the problems of supervision in libraries. In the general personnel management of libraries, supervision is an extremely difficult and sensitive subject and is becoming more so every day. In fact, the direct supervision of experienced professionals probably runs counter to the best ideals of the profession of librarianship. Once a professional librarian has passed a kind of probationary period, one in which the theory, skills and attitudes formed in the library school are modified by the demands of actual practice, and the librarian's abilities have been judged to be at least adequate for general performance, there shouldn't need to be any more direct day-to-day supervision. Since our profession is in transition, the difference between theory and practice in library supervision is substantial. It is best here, however, to discuss problems of supervision from a positive viewpoint.

Although comments here are made from the perspective of an academic librarian, I believe they are nevertheless pertinent to public libraries or library systems, wherever the structure is large enough to permit subdivision. Whether librarians are "tenured" or "protected by civil service" makes little difference. The common denominator is the librarian employed in his or her professional capacity; this is not limited to either academic or public libraries. In some libraries, professional librarians are not always treated as such; it is impossible to categorize the way people are treated by the kind of library in which they are employed.

Assuming, then, that our colleagues in tenured and other protected

1

positions don't need constant supervision, it seems that the library administrator's role is one of evaluating the quantity and quality of output, rather than the quantity and quality of daily work. One of the hallmarks of our profession is that, as individuals, we are able to approach reference questions, cataloging problems, acquisition puzzles and patron problems differently while producing results that are remarkably similar. This situation alone requires that there be parameters on the types of direct supervision that should be employed. The very nature of librarianship, i.e., the possibility of using different means for a given end — for instance, to achieve an adequate catalog record (now one that conforms to AACR2) — limits the kinds of supervision we can use.

Thus, along with the responsibility for training the people joining our profession, we are also responsible for dealing with those people, once they have been admitted as full colleagues, with a management style which respects their individual judgments, work habits, and methods of accomplishing assigned tasks. Not only is it theoretically better to operate in this fashion, it is probably the only method acceptable today. Any other approach will probably soon become increasingly unacceptable.

When one supervises through output evaluations, there is a hidden requirement that the task, be it cataloging, reference service, acquisitions or circulation, be one which can be measured. It is easier to measure quantity than quality, yet this is probably the less satisfactory of the two. However, it is the one employed most often in my experience, even by those supervisors who are trying to do the right thing. It is a dangerous choice. Another problem with supervision through use of output evaluations is the likelihood of long time lags between the performance of a task and the evaluation. In such situations, the good can go unrewarded and the bad uncorrected for extended periods of time.

There is also a problem of documentation — provision of the raw material from which to make the evaluation. This is probably easiest to obtain in the catalog departments, where traditionally every cataloger's work is evaluated, in the form of a revision, until that person has reached some level of competence (usually just after they've received their 25-year pins and are headed for the St. Petersburg Golden Age Home for Retired Librarians). Sometimes this evaluation takes the form of a review rather than a revision. After twenty years of librarianship, I've only just discovered the difference between review and revision. A review occurs when the supervisor insists on analyzing the cards *after* they have been filed rather than before. The reviewee must pull the cards if they are wrong. Review is considered more liberal than revision, which occurs when the cards pile up on the head cataloger's desk until he or she has had a chance to proofread each one. Reviews rather than revisions will take place for the senior members of the department. In departments other than cataloging, however, it is most likely that evaluation takes the form of an annual review of performance.

Reviews of a librarian's work are most likely done annually, because salaries are traditionally evaluated and budgets provided on an annual basis. This is not the case in all libraries, of course, but an annual review is the *least* that an employee should expect. An annual evaluation is the easiest to fit into other administrative demands, but it is probably a minimally satisfactory arrangement. More frequent evaluation is usually preferable. An enormous burden is therefore placed on the middle manager, since in most cases the library director will be unable to evaluate every person, and consequently unable to provide direct supervision, in any other than the smallest library. Thus, the task of the middle manager or "department head" is changing from supervision of departmental tasks to one of evaluation and quality control.

Evaluations should be performed in terms of the person being evaluated. In the end, one individual has to make the decision to say: "Yes, this is good work, the kind of performance we want to encourage"; or "No, this is a mediocre performance." In arriving at this decision, the evidence should include the perceptions of the person being evaluated. These evaluative decisions, which are, in fact, the supervising activity, are not of an "assembly line" nature — they are decisions which affect careers, and therefore the opinions and views of the people involved are quite important. In fact, they may be one of the most important aspects of job performance. There are cases when a person is obviously doing a good or bad job: a librarian who catalogs a book as educational psychology when it should have been classified as psychology of education is clearly in error. However, the way in which a librarian approaches a reference interview, circulation work or material selection has a lot to do with that librarian's perception of the work itself. Since those perceptions may be quite accurate, they should be brought into the evaluation.

A word of caution is in order here. Reference librarians, heads of cataloging, bibliographers and library directors are all personally responsible for a reasonable level of performance and are therefore accountable for that performance. One of the great dangers involved in the shared responsibility of participatory management is that those responsibilities might be ignored. I do realize, of course, that the people who talk about responsibility are usually library administrators who say "responsibility" means getting to work on time. However, the library administrator is also responsible and accountable, and his or her telling a subordinate to get to work on time is an attempt to live up to that responsibility. The responsibility is on both sides — on the answering of the reference question or the quality of the cataloging, as well as participating in evaluations. Not making evaluations is far more serious than not getting to work on time, not getting the cataloging done, or not answering a reference question completely.

One of our most common mistakes is the confusion of competence and enthusiasm. The library profession has had to undergo a great change from being an old-fashioned, authoritarian system, so that quite often we've proclaimed that we would accept anyone with the right attitudes. That problem is partially traceable to the library schools which gave priority to attitudinal change over solid training in professional skills. Although they are getting better at providing substantive education, many are still working under the burden of the past. In evaluation, it is not only attitude which is important, but also competence.

Enthusiasm and commitment are not librarianship itself — they only make good librarianship possible. These two qualities are not sufficient for good supervision, either. In evaluating job performance, a good supervisor doesn't report whether the person likes being a cataloger, but whether he or she is a good cataloger; not how well he or she likes being a bibliographer, but whether he or she can select one book over another; not how he or she feels about meeting people, but whether he or she is a good reference librarian. Recognizing these attributes of enthusiasm and commitment is part of the hiring process as well, but mistaking them for competence in evaluation can be disastrous.

The kind of supervision being discussed here — basically, the evaluation of one's colleagues' work — has several requisites. First, a written report either must be provided by the person being evaluated, or must come naturally out of his or her work. An example of such is an annual report. The importance of these reports for performance evaluation cannot be overemphasized, because they constitute the primary documentation for the evaluation. The monthly reports common in many businesses and nonprofit organizations are probably important for libraries as well and can provide the basis for more frequent evaluations. Very often the people most interested in evaluation and who frequently speak about governance and management are least likely to provide such documentation. They are the people who talk about the new programs for children but in their annual reports forget to note how many hours the library was open, whether or not the student assistants were paid, and how many reference questions were answered — all irritating details necessary for a full evaluation. A reference librarian probably hates to fill out forms every time he or she answers a question, or make the little marks that produce the statistics for that department. Nevertheless, that documentation is extremely valuable and as much a part of performance as the reference answer, the department's management, the cataloging, or the selection of books themselves. It should be remembered that these forms of documentation which provide the basis for the evaluation contain the perceptions of the writer as well as the facts. (Even the number of titles cataloged is occasionally, but not often, a question of perception.)

Also important in evaluating performance is the testimony of those served. For public libraries this includes the patrons and the city council; for academic libraries, the students and faculty; and for a library system, the member libraries. The reactions of these clients are an extremely valuable part of the evaluation, just as necessary as the annual or other periodic report. The role of the head of the library — or the personnel officer — should include compilation of this documentation in a logical fashion so that it can be used in conjunction with evaluations. Thus, one of the primary roles of the personnel office can be performed without interfering with the authority structure. I think all of us worry about past excesses in the use of personnel files, but without such files we return either to the situation where no evaluation of the institution takes place, or to one where such evaluations rest purely on the personal whim of the evaluator. While my suggestion may not be the best solution, a personnel file system, containing documents a person can examine and respond to, provides at least the basis for rational decision-making. When complaints are received, such as a letter saying, "Mr. Y misinformed me when I asked him about the train schedule from Hinsdale to Chicago. I went to the train station and found it didn't run on Saturday," Mr. Y can then indicate his reply, saying, "I thought he said Sunday." An evaluator can then see both sides of an issue.

Each time an evaluation takes place, it should include an interview with the person being evaluated. If the director or middle manager actually talks with the library employees once a year, it doesn't hurt either of them too much. They seldom transmit anything loathsome in those few minutes and I think that it serves a higher purpose. However, aside from concerns of social interaction, some record of the interview must be incorporated into the evaluation. Simply a nice talk between subordinate and supervisor is not sufficient — not just because of the traditional worry that the supervisor is saying nice things while acting on a bad evaluation, but more importantly because the only way to force people to make the evaluation at all is to insist that it be in writing. The problem is not that bad evaluations will occur, but rather that none will occur. Most of us will avoid making a negative statement about another person rather than perform our duty as a department head or even as a colleague. People are reluctant to say bad things because they don't want them to interfere with a personal relationship or with the smooth running of the library.

This negates the personal accountability of the supervisor or administrator. Our debt of accountability to society should be the overriding factor here.

Good performance must somehow be rewarded. In many highly structured systems, the reward for "barely acceptable" performance is often the same for "highly meritorious" work. I'm not certain what can be done in these situations, but to encourage good librarianship some kind of motivation must be provided. It may have to be outside the collective bargaining covenant or the civil service system, but some reward that says to the whole library that the person is an outstanding librarian — such as a better office or first claim to new furniture — has to occur. Public recognition of the good, the outstanding, the more-than-barely-adequate, is the positive reward that everyone has a right to expect as a professional, in this field or any other.

As I grow older, beyond the days when I thought of libraries as places for great intellectual and social change, the importance of simple housekeeping becomes increasingly apparent. Do not ignore the basic, daily library activity in the process of evaluation. Opening the doors on time and filing the catalog cards accurately are responsibilities of primary importance to our patrons, as are the hundreds of other basic library tasks. We may not have to perform these mundane tasks personally, but we must ensure that they are done. That is our personal responsibility: to do it right or to see that it is done right. Attention to these details is important because they allow the professional administrator to exist.

I will conclude by commenting on what I think are some of the effects of automation on supervision. Part of the documentation referred to here can or will be provided by various automated systems. Those machines will turn out statistical reports rapidly and efficiently, but the data may not really mean much. When LCS was installed at Ohio State University, one of the things it provided was an hour-by-hour, terminal-by-terminal statistical report on each type of command — a pile of paper two feet thick. I never read it; I always sent it to the systems analyst's office with a note saying, "Anything strange in this?" As far as I can tell, he never read it either, because he never replied. On the other hand, the statistical report of total activity by location was interesting because it could be used to assign more student assistants where needed, or — heaven forbid! — take some away from those libraries which reported that they were circulating a lot, while in some cases their circulation figures included reshelves. That is one of automation's advantages — it clarifies what is actually happening, and it is quite consistent. Automation will also eliminate many clerical tasks; that is, not clerks, but clerical *tasks*. This means there will be even less supervision taking place. Conferences such as this one may eventually be a waste of time, since the machine will do it all for us.

However, automation too has to be supervised. Supervision of machines requires the same evaluation as supervision of people — except you don't have to be nice to a machine. You will have to be nice to the computer center directors and the operators, because they may forget to turn on your system if you are not. Since the machine is not human, it will eliminate some problems of interpersonal relations. However, gleaning valuable information from the mass of statistics provided will be an additional problem in terms of the supervisory documentation.

One of the most important points to remember is that you can't use the computer as a scapegoat. It is simply not acceptable to decide not to renew any books this month "because the machine won't do it." Any librarian who delegates to the machine the basic responsibility for getting materials into the hands of patrons, analyzing those materials accurately, or selecting the right book, has failed. A basic relationship of automation to supervision is that the former cannot be used as an excuse by the latter. That supervision is important is unquestionably true; that its nature is changing is equally true.

LARS LARSON

Associate Professor
College of Business and Administration
Southern Illinois University at Carbondale

Contributions from the Theory of Administration Toward Understanding the Process of Supervision: Barth's Distinction

Barth's distinction is that there are two types of people: those who divide people into two types and those who don't.[1] This distinction is an appropriate one for the study of leadership, a field which consists of many dichotomies. Distinctions are made between leaders and subordinates, and appointed leaders and emergent leaders; between leadership and supervision, and management and leadership; and between leaders who are autocratic or democratic, boss-centered or subordinate-centered, and social-emotional or task-oriented.

The purpose of this paper is to focus on one of these distinctions: management as opposed to leadership. The literature on management indicates that only one aspect of management is concerned with leadership, and the leadership literature indicates little that is concerned with management. However, a review of literature on what managers actually do shows that aspects of management and leadership intertwine in the job of the supervisor. In focusing on the manager/leader distinction I will be concentrating on individuals who are appointed managers or leaders in a formal organization. This eliminates concern with emergent (informal) leaders and nonorganizational settings.

MANAGEMENT

In answer to the question, "What does a manager do?" the management literature is likely to contain some form of the acronym POSDCORB, which stands for:

> Planning, that is, working out in broad outline the things that need to be done and the methods for doing them to accomplish the purpose set for the enterprise;

9

Organizing, that is, the establishment of the formal structure of authority through which work subdivisions are arranged, defined, and coordinated for the defined objective;

Staffing, that is, the whole personnel function of bringing in and training the staff and maintaining favorable conditions of work;

Directing, that is, the continuous task of making decisions and embodying them in specific and general orders and instruction, and serving as leader of their enterprise;

Coordinating, that is, the all-important duty of interrelating the various parts of the work;

Reporting, that is, keeping those to whom the executive is responsible informed as to what is going on, which thus includes keeping himself and subordinates informed through records, research, and inspection; and

Budgeting, with all that goes with budgeting in the form of fiscal planning, accounting, and control.[2]

This description, or variations of it, has appeared in the management literature since the early 1900s and represents what managers *should* do. POSDCORB is based on managers' reflections about their jobs, and on attitude questionnaires administered and analyzed by scholars. Interestingly, only one of these seven aspects of a manager's job mentions leadership: the directing function includes decision-making, giving orders and overall leadership of the organization. A quick reading of the management literature gives the impression that leadership is a small component in the overall task of management. This traditional view of the manager's job draws heavily on measuring the end result in appraising performance. There is a tendency to add up wins and losses and assume that the manager is responsible for everything. This has led to the analogy of the manager as a symphony orchestra conductor, standing aloof on his platform while controlling the performance of the orchestra members.[3] Later in this paper I will stress the differences between what the literature says a manager *should* do and what managers *actually* do, and the difficulty in separating leadership actions from other aspects of managing. First, however, we need to take a brief look at the leadership literature.

LEADERSHIP

Leadership has traditionally been viewed as a subpart of managing and usually is defined in terms of influence. In a review of leadership research covering the period 1902-67, Stogdill found that almost all definitions suggest that leadership is an influence process.[4] A large body of research has concentrated on this influence process as it applies to face-to-face interactions between superiors and subordinates.

This research has been concerned with how superiors influence subordinates. For example, one study focused on the sources of power available to the leader in influencing followers. In a review of this power-influence process, Cartwright cites the following scheme developed by French and Raven:

> Reward power is based on P's* belief that O has the ability to mediate rewards for him. . . .
> Coercive power is based on P's belief that O has the ability to mediate punishments for him. . . .
> Referent power is based on P's identification with O. . . .
> Legitimate power stems from internalized values in P which dictate that O has a right to influence P and that P has an obligation to accept that influence. . . .
> Expert power is based on P's belief that O has some special knowledge or expertness.[5]

The more sources of power leaders have at their disposal, the more potential they have for influencing subordinates.

It is apparent that some of these sources of power stem from abilities and traits of the leader (i.e., expert and referent) and others from the situation in which the leader operates (i.e., does he or she possess the authority to hire, fire, give raises, etc.). Approaches to leadership based on the above scheme address the issue in terms of individual abilities and traits versus situational factors. Psychologists and sociologists have developed both trait theories and contingency theories of leadership. The trait theories attempt to identify personal characteristics of effective leaders that could be used in screening candidates for leadership positions. The contingency theories attempt to specify the conditions under which certain leader styles or behaviors are most effective.[6] Leadership research relies on a variety of methods, but laboratory studies focusing on specific aspects of leader behavior (i.e., how often an individual talks) and attitude surveys of leaders and their subordinates are the most common. Other papers in these proceedings will elaborate on alternate approaches to leadership study.

Leadership literature also treats leader effectiveness. The assumption has been made (though it has not been well tested) that by identifying personal traits associated with effectiveness and increasing our understanding of situational factors that influence effectiveness, an individual's leadership performance can be improved. In summary, leadership research has focused primarily on the face-to-face influence process between superior and subordinates and has attempted to identify personal and situational characteristics that enhance leader effectiveness.

---

* P denotes the agent subjected to influence and O denotes the agent exerting influence.

THE MANAGEMENT/LEADERSHIP DISTINCTION

I take the position of a person, to use Barth's distinction, that does not divide people into two types, and consequently argue that the manager/leader distinction is an artificial one that stands in the way of understanding the true nature of effective management, leadership or supervision. A cursory review of management literature indicates that leadership is only one aspect of the manager's job, and includes directing, making decisions and giving orders. In other words, leadership is directly influencing the individuals who comprise the organization. Leadership literature indicates that this influencing occurs in face-to-face interactions between leaders and followers. I suggest that, first, motivating and influencing others can and does occur in other than face-to-face superior/subordinate situations, and second, people tend to view a boss's job as a whole and typically do not distinguish between managerial and leadership aspects.

Each of the management functions has aspects that serve to influence individuals in the organization and thus overlaps the power-influence concept of leadership. Organizing, for example, involves work subdivisions and formal structure. In recent years considerable research has been done on job design and its impact on the performance and satisfaction of the individual performing that job.[7] The organizational structure can also influence performance of individuals. For example, Sayles suggests that: "The intragroup contacts between subordinates in a given managerial unit should be self-maintaining. That is, if the *organization structure* is correctly designed to facilitate the reintegration of division of jobs, subordinates act largely on the basis of stimuli provided by fellow subordinates." (Italics added.)[8]

Each of the leadership sources of power-influence has aspects that are part of the manager's job in other than the leader/follower relationship. Managers have to influence peers (other managers at the same level in the organization) as well as their bosses. The ability to help (reward) or not to help (punish) a peer can have an impact on the manager's performance in coordinating, staffing and reporting. Therefore, the many sources of power and influence that a leader can use with subordinates can also be used with peers and superiors in carrying out the management functions.

This suggests that the manager/leader dichotomy becomes blurred in practice. A person tends to be viewed as effective or ineffective in performing the job. It is very seldom that someone is said to be a good manager but a poor leader. In a study of chief executive officers, Mintzberg concluded that: "Leadership permeates all activities; its importance would be underestimated if it were judged in terms of the proportion of a manager's activities that are strictly related to leadership. . . . In virtually everything he does, the manager's actions are screened by subordinates searching for leadership clues."[9]

In summary, how a manager/leader designs jobs, organizes the structure of her or his unit, and influences peers and superiors has an impact on the individuals in that unit. To attempt to relate some of this impact to leadership and some to management is difficult and may not be useful in an attempt to increase understanding of our jobs.

NATURE OF A MANAGER'S JOB

In order to determine the skills and abilities necessary for effective job performance of managers, it is helpful to review what is known about the nature of a manager's work and the task demands placed on managers. The previous review of traditional management functions was based primarily upon survey research and interview methods of study. During the past several years, researchers have been reexamining these traditional assumptions by actually observing managers on the job or by having managers keep detailed diaries of their activities. Several characteristics of managerial work emerge from the results of these studies[10] that are helpful in identifying important managerial skills.

Managers are busy and work long hours. A manager's work week is typically between fifty and ninety hours. Those managers who work longer hours tend to be in higher-ranking positions in their organizations. Little free time is available and because of the open-ended nature of their jobs, they have a tendency to take work home.

Activities performed by managers are characterized by brevity, variety and fragmentation. Studies of activity rates (in which a new activity is recorded every time the manager changes the medium of his or her work, i.e., from meetings to telephone calls, tours, desk work, etc.) show as many as 500 activities per day for a foreman, and as few as 30 per day for a chief executive.

A foreman's activities range in length from a few seconds to two minutes. Higher-level managers average about nine minutes per activity. There is great variety in the activities performed and the trivial are interspersed with the important, requiring the manager to shift moods quickly and frequently. Interruptions and unplanned contacts are commonplace. Studies of top-level managers indicate that fifty to seventy such interruptions a day are not unusual. As a result, managers spend very little time alone. Studies indicate that executives average between one-half and one and one-half hours a day working alone, but this time is divided into brief periods of ten to fifteen minutes each. One study showed that an executive remained undisturbed at his desk for twenty-three minutes or more only twelve times in thirty-five days.

Verbal and written contacts are the manager's work. There are five discrete types of activity in which a manager engages: mail (or other paperwork), telephone, unscheduled or informal meetings, scheduled meetings, and inspection tours or visits.

Mail and paperwork take 22-36 percent of a manager's time. The manager generates much less mail than he or she receives and most of it is in response to incoming mail. The telephone is used for brief conversations and while it consumes a small proportion of a manager's time, it enables a manager to handle a large number of individual contacts. One study found that 36 percent of a manager's contacts were via the telephone. The scheduled meeting consumes more time than any other managerial activity — up to 60 percent. These meetings permit contacts of long duration with large groups of people. The manager's work is primarily oral. Studies indicate that 75-90 percent of a higher-level manager's time is spent in oral communication.

Information is a basic ingredient and contacts are all-important. There is strong support for the notion that the manager's major function is gathering information, and this activity may consume between 25 and 50 percent of the manager's time. In considering the process of getting information and passing it on to others, the total time spent on this activity exceeds 50 percent. Managers spend only 5-14 percent of their time making decisions and giving orders.

The manager has been likened to the neck of an hourglass, standing between his unit and a network of contacts. These contacts include superiors, peers and others who serve to inform the manager. Evidence indicates that as a person moves up the management hierarchy, the amount of time spent with individuals outside the manager's work group increases to one-half of his or her total working time. The majority of contacts outside the work group are with peers. Managers typically spend only 10-25 percent of their time with superiors.

IMPLICATIONS FOR TRAINING

At least two implications for management training can be drawn from the characteristics of a manager's job. The first concerns time management. Does a manager control the job or does the job control the manager? Current findings leave this issue unresolved. Some researchers believe that brevity, fragmentation and unplanned interruptions are the result of a flow of activities beyond the manager's control. They maintain that the manager has no choice but to respond to this flow. Others believe that managers thrive on and encourage interruptions and frequent changes of activities that lead to inefficient use of time, and argue that managers can do a better job of controlling how their time is spent. Given the large number of hours managers spend on the job and the open-ended nature of their work, training in time management should be of value.

The second implication concerns the amount of time managers spend in scheduled meetings. Studies show that managers may spend up to 60 percent of their time meeting regularly with other members of their organization. This suggests two potential training topics. First, training in the timing of meetings may be of value. Personal experiences tell us that many meetings are unnecessary. Often information can be obtained and issues resolved without formal meetings. Second, training in how to run a meeting may be useful. If considerable time is to be spent in meetings, effective leadership to improve the functioning of the group would be helpful.

In summary, improvement in at least three skill areas would be beneficial to a manager: training in time management, in the timing of meetings, and in effective management of meetings. Following are guides to this training taken from literature in the administrative sciences.

Time Management

An effective, straightforward approach to time management which can be done on an individual basis is keeping a diary. By keeping a diary of activities for a week or more, a manager can get immediate and direct feedback on how time is being spent. The diary should include type, duration and content of each activity and should be easy to fill out. It can provide information for answering such questions as:

1. Am I giving adequate attention to current activities, to reviewing the past and to planning for the future?
2. Am I dividing my time correctly between different aspects of my job? Is there, perhaps, one part of my job on which I spend too much time?
3. Have I allowed for the effects of changes which have taken place in the content of my job, my objective and in the organization of my work?
4. Am I doing work I ought to have delegated?
5. Who are the people I ought to be seeing? Am I spending too much or too little time with any of them?
6. Do I organize my working day and week according to priorities, or do I tend to deal with each problem as it turns up, without stopping to think whether there is something more important that I should be working on?
7. Am I able to complete a task or am I constantly interrupted? If the latter, are these interruptions an essential part of my work?[11]

As the studies of managers reviewed earlier in this paper indicate, much of a manager's time may not be controlled by the manager. This is all the more reason for a manager to look at how time is spent so that time within the manager's control can be used effectively.

When to Have a Meeting

In their approach to managerial decision-making, Victor Vroom and Philip Yetton provide a rational basis for answering the question, "Should I have a meeting?"[12] Their approach is based on the assumption that managers want to: (1) make good decisions, (2) have acceptance of their decision and a commitment to carry out the decision on the part of subordinates, and (3) minimize the time it takes to make a decision.

Below is the Vroom and Yetton model illustrating a structured approach to determining which type of decision-making method is most appropriate for a particular situation. Obviously, not all formal meetings a manager attends are solely for the purpose of problem-solving or decision-making. However, this model provides descriptions of a range of approaches to information-gathering as well as decision-making, and a set of diagnostic questions to guide the manager in deciding whether to have a meeting or make individual contacts with others in his or her unit. These following five approaches vary from autocratic to participative and represent a wide range of management styles.

(AI)* You solve the problem or make the decision yourself, using information available to you at that time.

(AII) You obtain the necessary information from your subordinates, then decide on the solution to the problem yourself. You may or may not tell your subordinates what the problem is in getting the information from them. The role played by your subordinates in making the decision is clearly one of providing the necessary information to you, rather than generating or evaluating alternative solutions.

(CI) You share the problem with relevant subordinates individually, getting their ideas and suggestions without bringing them together as a group. Then *you* make the decision which may or may not reflect your subordinates' influence.

(CII) You share the problem with your subordinates as a group, collectively obtaining their ideas and suggestions. Then *you* make the decision which may or may not reflect your subordinates' influence.

---

* The first letter of the symbol signifies the basic approach. *A* stands for autocratic, *C* for consultative, *G* for group. The roman numerals I and II represent individual and group approaches, respectively.

(GII) You share a problem with your subordinates as a group. Together you generate and evaluate alternatives and attempt to reach agreement (consensus) on a solution. Your role is much like that of chairman. You do not try to influence the group to adopt your solution and you are willing to accept and implement any solution which has the support of the entire group.[13]

Vroom and Yetton present seven diagnostic questions and a flow-chart (see Figure 1) to aid the manager in deciding which of the five decision-making styles is the most effective approach. To use the flow-chart, begin at the left side and ask the question in column A. If the answer is "no," proceed to column D. If the answer is "yes," move to column B, and so on. When a particular branch terminates the recommended management style is found.

How to Run a Meeting

Research indicates that there are two goals of group problem-solving: (1) achievement of a specific group task, and (2) maintenance or strengthening of the group itself. Leadership of the group is described in terms of task orientation and social-emotional orientation.[14] An extensive review of the literature on group leadership shows that:

1. task-oriented leadership is necessary for effective performance in all working groups;
2. acceptance of task-oriented leadership requires that the leader allow others to respond by giving feedback, making objections and questioning the leader;
3. social-emotional leadership orientation is required in addition to task-oriented leadership when groups are not engaged in satisfying or ego-involving tasks;
4. groups requiring both kinds of leadership behavior will be more effective when these behaviors are performed by one person rather than divided among two or more persons; and
5. when formally appointed leaders fail to perform behaviors required for group success, an informal leader will emerge and perform the necessary behaviors, provided that success is desired by the group members.[15]

These findings suggest that effective group functioning calls for some form of participative leadership on the part of the formal leader.

Maier suggests that effectiveness of meetings can be increased when leaders are trained to engage in the following leader behaviors: (1) sharing of information with members; (2) preventing dominant personalities

FIGURE 1. DECISION PROCESS FLOW-CHART

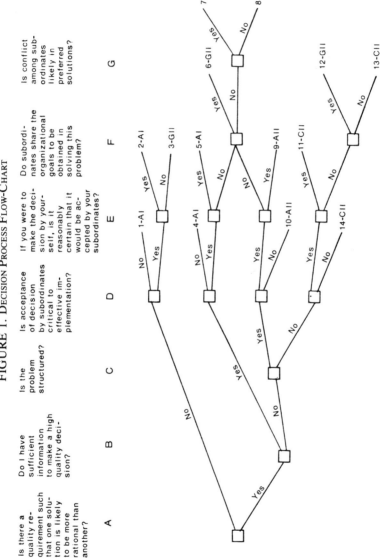

Source: Reprinted, by permission of the publisher, from "A New Look at Managerial Decision Making," by Victor H. Vroom, *Organizational Dynamics*, Spring 1973, p. 70, © 1973 by AMACOM, a division of American Management Associations. All rights reserved.

from having undue influence; (3) soliciting opinions, facts and feelings from reticent members; (4) assisting members in communicating with each other; (5) protecting deviant opinions from being rejected without fair evaluation; (6) minimizing blame-oriented statements; (7) redirecting unfocused discussion back to the problems; (8) encouraging alternative solutions; (9) delaying the evaluation of alternatives until all have been presented; and (10) guiding the process of the selection of the best alternative.[16] It is evident from this list of behaviors that a participative leader does not abdicate the role of leadership. The role of the participative leader is one of obtaining relevant information, expertise and commitment to implementation of the chosen solution.

SUMMARY

This paper began with a brief review of the traditional views of management and leadership and suggested that a distinction between them was not helpful in understanding the task of motivating, supervising or managing subordinates. Management and leadership roles are so intertwined in practice that only an understanding of the nature of the manager's task demands can provide clues to the skills necessary for effective management/leadership. A review of findings about the nature of a manager's job suggests at least three skill areas that managers should master: (1) management of time, (2) timing of meetings, and (3) how to run a meeting. Specific findings from research in these areas along with guidelines for training were provided.

REFERENCES

1. Schneiker, Conrad. "An Abridged Collection of Interdisciplinary Laws," *The CoEvolution Quarterly*, no. 8, Winter 1975, p. 138.
2. Mintzberg, Henry. *The Nature of Managerial Work*. New York, Harper & Row, 1973, p. 9. *See also* Gulick, Luther H. "Notes on the Theory of Organization." *In* Luther H. Gulick and L.F. Urwick, eds. *Papers on the Science of Administration*. New York, Columbia University Press, 1937, pp. 1-45.
3. Carlson, Sune. *Executive Behaviour: A Study of the Work Load and Working Methods of Managing Directors*. Stockholm, Strömbergs, 1951, p. 52.
4. Stogdill, Ralph M. *Handbook of Leadership: A Survey of Theory and Research*. New York, Free Press, 1974.
5. Cartwright, Dorwin. "Influence, Leadership, Control." *In* James G. March, ed. *Handbook of Organizations*. Chicago, Rand McNally, 1965, pp. 28-30. *See also* French, J.R.P., Jr., and Raven, B. "The Bases of Social Power." *In* Dorwin Cartwright, ed. *Studies in Social Power*. Ann Arbor, University of Michigan, Institute for Social Research, 1959, pp. 118-49.

6. Korman, Abraham. "Contingency Approaches to Leadership: An Overview." *In* James G. Hunt and Lars L. Larson, eds. *Contingency Approaches to Leadership.* Carbondale, Southern Illinois University Press, 1974, pp. 189-98.

7. Hackman, J. Richard. "Work Design: Behavioral Science Approaches to Organizational Change." *In* J. Richard Hackman and J. Lloyd Suttle, eds. *Improving Life at Work.* Santa Monica, Calif., Goodyear, 1977, pp. 96-162.

8. Sayles, Leonard R. *Managerial Behavior.* New York, McGraw-Hill, 1964, p. 52.

9. Mintzberg, op. cit., p. 61.

10. McCall, Morgan, et al. *Studies of Managerial Work: Results and Methods* (Technical Report No. 9). Greensboro, N.C., Center for Creative Leadership, 1978, pp. 6-18; and Mintzberg, op. cit., pp. 51-53.

11. Stewart, Rosemary. "Diary Keeping as a Training Tool for Managers," *Journal of Management Studies* 5:295-303, Oct. 1968; and _____. *Managers and Their Jobs.* London, Macmillan, 1967, pp. 146-47.

12. Vroom, Victor H., and Yetton, Philip W. *Leadership and Decision-Making.* Pittsburgh, University of Pittsburgh Press, 1973.

13. Vroom, Victor H. "A New Look at Managerial Decision-making." *In* David A. Kolb, et al., eds. *Organizational Psychology: A Book of Readings.* 2d ed. Englewood Cliffs, N.J., Prentice-Hall, 1974, p. 65.

14. Bales, Robert F. "Task Roles and Social Roles in Problem-solving Groups." *In* Eleanor E. Maccoby, et al., eds. *Readings in Social Psychology.* 3d ed. New York, Holt, Rinehart & Winston, 1958, pp. 437-47.

15. House, Robert J., and Baltz, Mary. "Leadership: Some Empirical Generalizations and New Research Directions" (Working Paper 78-02). Toronto, Ont., University of Toronto, 1978, pp. 28-29.

16. Maier, Norman R. *Problem Solving and Creativity in Individuals and Groups.* Belmont, Calif., Brooks-Cole, 1970.

RICHARD J. VORWERK
Dean of Special Programs
and Instructional Services
Governors State University
Park Forest South, Illinois

The Research Basis of Employee-Centered Supervision

As supervisors in libraries, our job is to achieve, through the efforts of others, those results for which we are responsible. On the surface, the task appears to be relatively simple. However, if we were aware of all the variables involved and had control of them, there would be no need for conferences like this Allerton institute.

As supervisors, we are fully aware that unknown variables influence the supervisory process and that, even when variables are known, we do not always know how to handle them. Managing people in a library or any other organization can be a very tenuous affair. One of the main purposes of interludes such as this conference in our busy work schedule is to provide an opportunity to step back from the activities that constitute a major portion of our lives and reflect on their meaning. We must understand them in order to perform effectively. The volume and complexity of the work that must be done make it impossible for us to complete it all and to achieve all the desired results.

Supervision is by no means a new activity, but it has only recently been investigated in a meaningful fashion. Libraries are one example of the developing organizations that brought out the need to approach supervision in a more systematic manner. At the turn of the century, theorists first concentrated on the task to be performed as one of the major variables to be considered in any study of supervision. Frederick Taylor's theory of scientific management exemplified this approach.[1] The next variable to come under scrutiny was human relations, which brought to light factors that intervened significantly in the work process. Interest in this area was stimulated by the Hawthorne studies conducted by a group

21

of Harvard sociologists at the Western Electric Company's Hawthorne Works near Chicago.[2] The recognition of these two variables defined an area which could be researched with the possibility that conclusive findings could be applied to influence behavior in actual work situations.

Studying management or supervision is like studying metaphysics in that, as Aristotle remarked 2000 years ago, 40 is an appropriate age to begin since experience is an essential ingredient. Management is an art, not just a science, and good results are obtained only when knowledge and action are combined. Thus, valid research findings must necessarily be of great help to the successful supervisor.

The way we learn, or should learn, to supervise will partially explain the role of research in supervision. The basis of all learning and decision-making is experience.[3] The experience on which we base our understanding of a situation or problem in order to learn or make decisions is inherent. In the attempt to understand, insights are gained. To determine whether or not these insights are true, we hearken back to past experience. True judgments about the underlying realities of this past experience are the basis for good decisions. The validity of such decisions can only be verified by experience. Theories are used to organize our experience into meaningful patterns so that we can understand the supervisory process and predict (with some probability of success) what course of action will obtain the desired results most effectively and efficiently.

We can all improve our supervisory talents. The first thing to do is raise our level of consciousness and become aware of what is happening with regard to the supervisory process. Research is the formal tool allowing us to verify the judgments of management theorists. Decisions based on these judgments are subject to the same review.

THE UNIVERSITY OF MICHIGAN STUDIES

Rensis Likert performed a set of studies at the University of Michigan which were primarily concerned with discovering the principles and methods of effective leadership.[4] The studies were conducted in a wide variety of industries and data were collected from thousands of employees.

Two distinct styles of supervision were identified: job-centered and employee-centered. The job-centered leader closely supervises subordinates so that they perform their tasks using only specified procedures. Coercion, reward and legitimate power are used to influence their behavior and performance. Concern for people is viewed as necessary, but is not always taken into consideration. The employee-centered leader, on the other hand, believes in delegating decision-making and in helping followers satisfy their needs by providing a supportive work environment. He or she is also concerned with the personal growth and achievement of subordinates.

These two behavioral styles were tested by Morse and Reimer in a study involving more than 500 clerical employees for a period of one year.[5] These employees were located in four divisions which were organized in a similar manner, used the same kind of technology, did much the same kind of work, and employed similar kinds of people. In two divisions, job-centered supervision was used for the one-year period, and in the other two, employee-centered supervision. During that time, production output was measured continually. Supervisor and employee attitudes, perceptions and other variables were measured before and after the experimental year.

Production under both systems increased about equally. However, under employee-centered supervision, the employees themselves reduced the size of the work force and developed many procedural changes which helped increase productivity. The satisfaction indicators (e.g., absenteeism, turnover and attitudes) also improved. In the job-centered divisions, rewards and promotions were integrated mainly with production results, which helped attain short-term improvement but which could become counterproductive in the long run. The conclusion reached here, and by Likert and other researchers involved in similar studies, is that employee-centered supervision is more effective.

Likert's studies at Michigan led him and his coworkers to postulate System 4, a theory aimed at integrating all our experiences as supervisors into a whole. This in turn would enable us (1) to formulate yet more research, and (2) to supervise, knowing that at least some practice has been verified.[6] The whole notion of organizational development is based on the assumption that an organization's most important resource is the people who function within it. As they develop, the theory goes, it is probable that organizational objectives will be achieved more effectively.

THE OHIO STATE UNIVERSITY STUDIES

Another significant research study on leadership was conducted at Ohio State University after World War II.[7] This study was based on a 2-factor theory of leadership: initiating structure and consideration. Initiating structure refers to a supervisor's behavior of organizing and defining work-group relationships as well as establishing well-defined channels of communication. In this model, the means of getting a job done are defined by the supervisor, not the work-group members. Consideration refers to behavior in which friendship, mutual trust and rapport exist between supervisor and employees. These two factors were used to describe leadership behavior in organizational settings. The researchers sought to assess supervisors' perceptions of their own optimum behavior in leadership roles as well as employee perceptions of supervisory behavior.

Part of the study compared supervisors with different consideration and initiating structure scores in terms of various performance measures. These performance measures were obtained from proficiency ratings made by plant management and included other factors such as unexcused absenteeism, accidents, formally filed grievances, and employee turnover. Data on these variables were gathered for an 11-month period for each supervisor's work group.

Supervisors who worked in production divisions were compared to supervisors in nonproduction divisions. In the production divisions there was a positive correlation between proficiency and initiating structure and a negative correlation between consideration and proficiency. The findings were reversed in the nonproduction divisions.

In extrapolating these findings to libraries, proficient technical services supervisors ought to score high on initiating structure, and proficient public services supervisors should score high on consideration. However, studies also concluded that high initiating structure and low consideration scores correlated with greater absenteeism, accidents, grievances and turnover.

THE CONTINGENCY LEADERSHIP MODEL

The third study to be considered is that which Fiedler conducted over a decade ago at the University of Illinois at Urbana-Champaign.[8] The model he developed and researched hypothesized that leadership is a relationship based on power and influence, and that group performance is dependent on the interaction of leadership style and situation favorableness. Two questions were formulated to address the influence of these two variables. The first concerns the degree to which the situation provides the supervisor with the power and influence needed to be effective, and the second questions the extent to which supervisors can predict the effects of their leadership styles on the performance and behavior of employees.

Three situational factors were proposed which would influence a supervisor's effectiveness: leader/member relations, task structure and position power. The interpersonal relationships between supervisor and employees are considered to be the most important variable. This factor reflects the acceptance of the supervisor and is measured in two ways: (1) a sociometric preference scale on which employees indicate whether they accept a superior, and (2) a group atmosphere scale which consists of ten 8-point items to be answered by employees.

The second most important measure of situation favorableness is task-structure. This variable includes the following components: goal clarity, goal-path multiplicity, decision verifiability, and decision specificity. These four components indicate the degree to which employees' jobs are either routine or nonroutine. Goal clarity refers to the group members' understanding of a task's requirements. Goal-path multiplicity is an index of the degree to which the task can be completed by various procedures, methods or alternate solutions. Decision verifiability targets the degree to which appropriateness of the solution can be demonstrated either by appeal to authority, logical procedures or feedback. Finally, decision specificity refers to the degree to which there may be more than one correct solution. (For instance, in cataloging there may be only one correct main entry, while there may be a multitude of ways to answer a reference question.)

The third situational factor is position power and refers to the power inherent in the leadership or supervisory position. This variable includes the rewards and punishments usually associated with the position, the official authority based on ranking in the hierarchy, and the support that the supervisor receives from superiors and the overall organization.

Leadership style is measured by evaluating supervisor responses to a Least-Preferred Coworker (LPC) questionnaire. Supervisors who rate their least-preferred coworker in favorable terms (high LPC) are identified as people-oriented and supportive. Those supervisors who give low LPC ratings are considered more task-oriented.

By using his 3-dimensional model, LPC scores and research findings, Fiedler postulated that job-centered supervisors function best in certain types of situations and employee-centered supervisors function best in others. Thus, a manager's effectiveness can be improved by assignment to a situation that is appropriate to his or her managerial style. For example, a supervisor in a structured situation with a strong position of power who has a good relationship with the work group should find that a job-centered style would be effective. Supervisors of catalog card production units in large academic libraries, who are popular with their employees and whose word is law, could use a very directive managerial style that emphasizes task completion and expect both effective and efficient results. On the other hand, a supervisor with an unstructured task to perform, a weak position of power, and only a moderately good relationship with the work groups, would be more effective with an employee-centered style.

Fiedler and Chemers advocate engineering the situation to fit the style of the supervisors.[9] Supervisor/employee relations can be restructured to make background, educational level or technical expertise more compatible. Unions and civil service rules, however, can make this kind of adjustment difficult. Tasks can be made more structured by precisely spelling out the details of the job, and less structured by providing only general instructions. Supervisor position power can also be modified in many ways, e.g., a higher rank in the organization or more authority to do the job can be given.

Fiedler does not advocate leadership training.[10] In fact, his own studies indicate that such training is not effective, that supervisors with a lot of training perform about as well as those with little or no training. The practical suggestions offered by the results of Fiedler's research may not be feasible in every organizational setting, including libraries. Reality has a way of thwarting the implementation of possible situational changes.

A more recent set of studies deals with the path-goal theory which suggests the four different leadership styles that can be and are being used by supervisors: directive, supportive, participative and achievement-oriented.[11] The path-goal theory assumes that these four styles are used by the same leader in different situations. The directive style of leadership is characterized by the assigning of particular tasks, specifying of procedures and scheduling of work. The supportive leader reduces frustrating barriers to task completion, especially in times of stress. The participative style can be recognized by the subordinate's involvement with the leader in task assignment, procedure specification and work scheduling. The achievement-oriented leader is more concerned with the task to be completed than with the feelings and expectations of subordinates. As this theory is relatively new, there have only been a limited number of studies testing its assumptions.

The last model to be considered here is the Vroom and Yetton Model.[12] The purpose of this model is to identify the appropriate leadership style for particular situations. The leadership styles are defined in terms of subordinate participation in decision-making. At one end of the model spectrum, the leadership style specifies that the leader will make the decision, and at the other end, that the leader and the rest of the work group will arrive at a consensus decision. A matrix has been developed using five leadership styles and seven key situational questions, answers to which indicate the appropriate leadership behavior. While the research findings on this model are not yet available, the theory has a certain attractiveness to practicing supervisors who are looking for training to aid them in becoming more effective.

CONCLUSION

The practical conclusions that can be drawn from the research findings concerning job-centered and employee-centered supervision are not entirely conclusive. However, the spectrum of both situations and leadership styles, ranging from job-centered to employee-centered, accommodate most of us.

In libraries, as in other organizations, we should learn what styles we are capable of using. Even though we may have a propensity to exhibit one style rather than another, most of us are able to adjust to different situations and interpersonal relationships. The art of supervision, then, first calls for an awareness of oneself and one's leadership style. Then we must become aware of the relevant needs of employees and the significant factors in the job situation. Effective supervision requires appropriate adjustment to employees, situations, particular tasks and oneself. Supervision is a creative act in which we participate to bring about desired results. To be effective supervisors, we need to use the research findings that have been verified in order to improve our own effectiveness.

REFERENCES

1. Taylor, Frederick W. *The Principles of Scientific Management.* New York, Harper and Bros., 1911. (Reprinted by W.W. Norton & Co., 1967.)
2. Roethlisberger, Fritz J., and Dickson, William J. *Management and the Worker.* Cambridge, Mass., Harvard University Press, 1939.
3. Lonergan, Bernard J. *Insight: A Study of Human Understanding.* 3d ed. New York, Philosophical Library, 1970.
4. Likert, Rensis. *New Patterns of Management.* New York, McGraw-Hill, 1961.
5. Morse, Nancy C., and Reimer, Everett. "The Experimental Change of a Major Organizational Variable," *Journal of Abnormal and Social Psychology* 52:120-29, 1956.
6. Likert, Rensis. *The Human Organization.* New York, McGraw-Hill, 1967.
7. Fleishman, Edwin A., et al. *Leadership and Supervision in Industry; An Evaluation of a Supervisory Training Program* (Monograph No. 33). Columbus, Bureau of Educational Research, Ohio State University, 1955.
8. Fiedler, Fred E. *A Theory of Leadership Effectiveness.* New York, McGraw-Hill, 1967.
9. _____, and Chemers, Martin M. *Leadership and Effective Management.* Glenview, Ill., Scott, Foresman & Co., 1974.
10. Fiedler, Fred E. "The Leadership Game: Matching the Man to the Situation," *Organizational Dynamics* 4:6-16, Winter 1976.
11. House, Robert J. "A Path Goal Theory of Leader Effectiveness," *Administrative Science Quarterly* 16:321-38, Sept. 1971.
12. Vroom, Victor H., and Yetton, Philip W. *Leadership and Decision-Making.* Pittsburgh, University of Pittsburgh Press, 1973.

MARTHA J. BAILEY
Physics Librarian
Purdue University
West Lafayette, Indiana

An Overview of Supervision in Libraries Today

The literature of library and information management is often of little assistance to the professional who supervises. Interactions with departments and services of the parent organization, such as conforming to policies on personnel, purchasing or accounting, are seldom clarified. Some of the literature reports management theories which were developed for business organizations. However, these theories may not be applicable to libraries, since libraries do not have the same types or levels of personnel, are not organized in the same way, and cannot amortize equipment or take advantage of other tax features which companies utilize. The authors of literature on management theory warn that, because of differences in the way companies are organized and operated, it can be dangerous to borrow concepts or ideas that worked in one company and apply them to another. In fact, even the designations "top management," "middle management" and "supervisory management" signify different concepts in different companies and libraries.[1]

The area of supervisory management requires particular caution. In any organization, it is at this level that policies are implemented. This paper uses the rather broad definition of supervision as the face-to-face interaction of a library professional, who has administrative responsibility, with another employee, usually a subordinate. This applies at all levels of management with all types of employees: to the director interacting with assistant directors, to the department head with his or her professionals, or to the professional with clerical employees.

Both management literature and the library literature are written as if management were pure, pristine, and conducted in a leisurely manner.

One author recently discussed the "managerial mystique," claiming that management is mathematical in rationale, steeped in business jargon, male in orientation, and predicated on assumptions about power relationships.[2] The literature acknowledges little of the rush, conflict or indecision of the actual job situation. One branch librarian in a public library recently told me that he had difficulty remembering theory X or Y when two employees were coming to blows. In libraries, as in industry, decisions are not always logical, clear-cut and accepted by all concerned.

Why is there concern about supervision? The answer is economics. Fry and White stated that in 1973, salaries accounted for 59 percent of academic libraries' budgets, 68 percent of public libraries' budgets, and 60-65 percent of special libraries' budgets.[3] The University of Illinois's 1977 annual survey of public libraries indicated that 67 percent of budgeted funds were for salaries.[4]

The topic of supervision is a particularly sensitive one for those in the library and information field. The supervisor may feel that he or she is an example of the Peter Principle, viz., that people rise in an organization to their maximum level of incompetence. In supervision, it is more likely that Murphy's Law operates: anything that can go wrong will. Studies indicate that librarians have poor leadership qualities, exhibit little interest in administration, and are poor managers.[5] In a session on middle management at ALA's 1978 conference in Chicago, the first question from the floor was, "Why are librarians such poor managers and supervisors?" It has only been in recent years that "bad news" stories have begun to appear,[6] but today almost every issue of *Library Journal* contains at least one news story about a library's administrative problems.[7]

However, despite obvious major differences between industrial and library management, there are similarities:

1. In both the company and the library, supervisors must learn to supervise. This skill is not intuitive, but can be developed through study, observation and practice.
2. Both companies and libraries are haunted by the phantom of the "happy employee." For years sociologists and psychologists have said that people must enjoy their jobs. Now some writers are providing contrary views.[8]
3. Both companies and libraries use different styles of supervisory management for different work settings and types of employees. Corporations use different techniques and styles for employees in production, research and sales; for professional and nonprofessional employees; and for various combinations of classifications. In libraries there are professional, nonprofessional, student, public service, library faculty,

processing, and branch library employees, all of which are treated in a slightly different manner.

4. Both companies and libraries have employees who are considered to be problems for one reason or another. These "problem employees" may be found at all levels of the organization.

This paper outlines some of the components of library supervisory management today. In 1977 I prepared a review on the special librarian as a supervisor and middle manager.[9] The present paper will touch a few of the same points, but will include new material, partly based on a survey of recent library school graduates.

THE LIBRARY ENVIRONMENT

In order to gain some perspective on the milieu in which supervisory management takes place, one must look at the library environment. In this regard, Echelman cites factors such as the "structure, personnel, products, policies, plans, and the political interaction of people and departments" of the parent organization.[10] Librarians are classified as supervisors or middle managers according to the academic, administrative or public civil service classifications. Library faculty members may be expected to meet the same requirements for research and publication that teaching faculty members are.

The review on the special librarian as supervisor includes detailed descriptions of academic, public, institutional, government, special, and other library environments.[11] Academic libraries have provosts, boards of trustees and influential alumni. Their library committees for the system and for the individual branch libraries are composed of faculty. These tax-supported libraries are also governed by the state legislature and sometimes by a board of regents or commission on higher education. In addition to reporting to a local official, public libraries usually have boards of trustees which represent the citizens. Some public libraries also receive funds from state legislatures.

There are also library/information services for state and federal agencies and for companies and corporations. There are libraries in hospitals, museums, prisons and nursing homes, and library/media centers in the schools. A new type of library is the administrative headquarters of networks or consortia. Each of these has its own separate "environment."

INTERACTIONS OF LIBRARY PERSONNEL

In the library environment, interactions between library personnel take place on many different levels. Often one thinks of the above-mentioned groups interacting with the library director or assistant director, but generally interactions originate at lower levels in the organization. For example, the interlibrary loan librarian at the public library may be asked by a local company representative to use the library teletype, the only one in the community. An influential alumnus may request the branch librarian to provide him or her with a receipt for books donated to the library for tax credit purposes. The irate citizen who objects to materials in the collection usually approaches the circulation supervisor first. These examples indicate the need for guidelines, particularly written guidelines, that will enable supervisors to cope with situations as they arise.

There are positive interactions to consider as well. Circulation supervisors are often requested to attend a library board meeting when circulation is to be discussed. Supervisors may give presentations at budget reviews and other key meetings. The branch heads perform a great many liaison activities, with the community in a public library or with the subject departments in a university.

Whether they are in public, government agency, academic or company situations, library managers have similar relationships with other departments in the parent organization which affect their decisions. For example, the parent organization may insist that all purchasing be processed by the central purchasing department rather than permit the library acquisitions supervisor to send orders directly to the vendors. This sometimes causes delays without any appreciable financial benefits since some types of book and subscription orders allow very little discount. Many tax-supported agencies must solicit bids for orders; this sometimes impedes the development of continuing services with vendors. Other complications arise when the central purchasing department specifies the manufacturers from which equipment such as typewriters or photocopiers may be purchased.

Other departments in the parent organization with which library supervisory personnel must interact include personnel departments, central business offices, computer service centers, subject departments, and building and maintenance services. The central business office is also usually involved in issuing paychecks and budgeting for expenditures, and large library systems often have a staff accountant to deal with the central business office. Library supervisors must also interact with the central computer service, e.g., the systems librarian sometimes must consult with the computer center on selection of software programs, and library management's needs for data must be scheduled at the computer center. Even the building and maintenance service sometimes affects decisions of library managers. Staff changes and clientele services may be delayed until custodial staff move furniture or electricians install equipment. Smoking or eating may be prohibited in some areas by building regulations.

An important issue in supervisory management is the amounts of time which should be devoted to supervision and to serving the clientele. This is an especially difficult problem in libraries which are open long hours, as the administration may not be able to provide professional assistance during the entire time that the public service areas are open. Supervisors of branch or departmental libraries often do not have sufficient professional help to provide reference service at all hours, which is particularly unfortunate in a specialized subject department. However, supervisors must be available between 9:00 a.m. and 5:00 p.m., the standard workday of many organizations.

Some administrators solve these dilemmas by having the department head assume all supervision, freeing other professionals to interact with clientele. Another solution is for the department head to assign one professional to supervise clerks. Such responsibilities may also be rotated in order to give all the professionals supervisory experience.

There are sometimes auxiliary or even competing library and information services on the same property, or funded by the same organization. University and public libraries are involved with research institutes, independent laboratories, instructional centers, or computer-based instruction centers, all of which may employ parent organization personnel or draw extensively on the collections.

The new free-lance service, offered on a fee basis, often utilizes the collections of nearby university or public libraries.[12] These services include on-line computer searches, document delivery, consultation, and others which parallel or supplement standard library services.

The network or consortium authority is now beginning to influence the work of supervisory managers in its member libraries. The interlibrary loan supervisor who depended on personal contacts in neighboring libraries to obtain fast service must now conform to formulas established by the consortium. The chief cataloger has the original cataloging of his department scrutinized by all members of the on-line computer cataloging network.[13] All administrators are involved in motivating employees to adapt to innovations associated with joining a network or consortium.[14]

MANAGEMENT OF LIBRARIES AND INFORMATION SERVICES

The primary reason that interest in library management has been gathering momentum in recent years is due to the problems of providing services to all types of clientele in the face of increased inflation and reduced budgets. The emphasis on the functional form of organization has been spurred by Association of Research Libraries studies and the development of its Management Review and Analysis Program.[15]

Large, multicampus systems, such as those in Indiana, California and New York, must adapt to: (1) the prevailing wages in each community; (2) the number and abilities of people available to fill the positions; (3) the number of hours the library is open, which is based on the commuting patterns of students, faculty and employees; (4) the types of courses taught; and (5) the amount and types of research conducted. Due to the interdisciplinary nature of subject fields and the cost of maintaining separate facilities, there has been a trend away from multibranch, specialized or departmental systems in universities. In the public library, costs are halting the trend toward specialized branches for subject and clientele.

Libraries are complex organizations, and the larger the library, the greater its complexity. As part of the trend toward scientific management and the use of on-line computer systems, new professional positions — which are sometimes not held by professional librarians — have arisen. These include accountants, personnel people, systems analysts and subject specialists who work with collection development or on-line searches. Many librarians believe the only "true" librarian is one with background in the humanities or social sciences; they even exclude those trained in life sciences, physical sciences and mathematics. These conflicting definitions of "professional" may interfere with daily working relationships.

LIMITATIONS ON LIBRARY MANAGEMENT

Many factors can adversely affect the supervisor's authority. Sometimes library employees are assigned responsibilities without the authority to take appropriate action. For example, the branch head may have several levels of the hierarchy to which he or she must report:

> An academic library may have many physically separate service points, but little decentralization, if the branch librarians are not delegated authority to undertake meaningful independent actions. . . . Scientific management . . . demands that the degree of decentralization . . . be decided on the basis of . . . such factors as the need for uniform policies, the relative economics of library size and location, the availability of personnel with managerial ability or potential, and the effectiveness of the control techniques available to the delegating manager.[16]

As mentioned above, the library's membership in networks and consortia may also limit the decisions of the individual supervisor; a recent article notes some of the tension networks can create for the participating libraries.[17] Referring to the business management literature, Petit states that the industrial supervisor must operate in a highly intradependent organization and interact with many different individuals who, directly or indirectly, affect his or her job. The supervisor must make five major accommodations:

1. ideological (the supervisor is no longer "boss");
2. engineering (in industry, the engineering department tells the foreman what products to make and how to make them);
3. personnel (staff departments have taken over functions such as hiring, placement, training, transferring, awarding merit increases, and firing);
4. organization-systems (other staff members establish procedures and techniques such as planning, operations research, finance and accounting); and
5. labor-relations (the supervisor must contend with a union steward who represents his subordinates).[18]

There are many parallels in the library. The personnel function seems to be changing most rapidly. Ruth Jackson reports that prior to 1970, academic libraries lagged in the areas of job analysis, job evaluation and personnel testing.[19] The complexities of hiring in accordance with equal opportunity strictures and the emphasis on staff development will possibly bring even greater attention to this area. In the organization-systems accommodation, as the operations become more mechanized, the services are adapted to the system. For example, use of OCLC tapes to produce accessions lists for the branch libraries may limit the amount and kinds of individualized material that can be included in these lists. A problem inherent in the shift from the hierarchical organization in the library is that professionals must consider whether they should give priority to obeying the administrators or to fulfilling responsibility (i.e., providing service to clientele).[20]

Another pervasive problem is enforcing directives. Rules state that students cannot work unless they have an employment form on file; however, in emergencies supervisors may hire a temporary substitute just to keep a branch open. During the winter storms of 1978, Purdue University issued directives that employees who did not report for work had to take vacation time or other accrued leave in order to be paid; however, many supervisors unofficially permitted employees to make up the time.

The literature concerning the leadership qualities of librarians and information specialists is extremely negative. Binder has studied the supervisory behavior of librarians in academic libraries and found that there was little difference between professional and nonprofessional employees' abilities for and attitudes toward supervision.[21] In a study of middle managers in medium-sized public libraries, Gamaluddin found that professionals were unwilling to make decisions even when they were given the opportunity to do so.[22]

Kay's analysis of industrial managers closely parallels the situation for middle managers in libraries and information services. Many persons who entered middle management in the 1960s now find they are boxed in by their jobs; they are too specialized for lateral transfer or they lack the varied work experiences and formal education required for advancement. They suffer from job insecurity, lack of authority, career inflexibility, and threat of obsolescence. As with supervisors, increased interest in scientific management only creates more tensions. Although controls and systems provide middle managers with information on which to base decisions, these same controls have the effect of increasing the visibility of all successes and failures and thus may increase pressures to perform better.[23]

There has been much discussion about faculty status for academic librarians but little substantive material on how the librarian is to devote adequate time to publication and research as well as perform administrative responsibilities. When a teaching faculty member takes a sabbatical, the department does not offer his or her courses in the interim. If a library faculty member takes a sabbatical, however, someone must assume those responsibilities during that period.[24] Another implication of faculty status is that the library faculty forms a "collegial body" and should select its own head, who may not necessarily be the library director.[25] Bailey points out questions that arise when a collegial organization is superimposed over a library organization.[26]

PROBLEMS FACING THE LIBRARY SUPERVISOR

In the following sections some items concerning the direct supervision of employees are considered: the composition of the work force, the question of motivation and staff development, and some implications of collective bargaining and equal opportunity for employment.

Nonprofessional Personnel

The advent of technical assistants and aides in libraries has raised the 2-fold problem of "career ladders": (1) years of experience substitute for a master's degree in library science in the case of the nonprofessional,[27] and (2) auxiliary employees, such as nonsupervisory professionals and research systems and personnel staff, have pay scales and status equated with those of library supervisors.

In some organizations, flexible scheduling or flex-time is used.[28]

This takes two principal forms: (1) staff may work any hours they choose for a total of thirty-five to forty hours per week, or (2) they may work ten hours per day, four days per week with three days off. An inherent problem with this innovation is ensuring that sufficient personnel to handle the daily work load are present. Schemes such as this have arisen in order to staff computer operations or attract personnel who would normally be unable to work a standard day due to family commitments, class schedules or other personal reasons. Although public service units have always had some scheduling flexibility due to the long hours they are open, these schemes provide even greater flexibility.

Many areas of the country are experiencing a severe shortage of clerical and secretarial people. Reasons for this are varied: women are seeking jobs in other fields, and companies are giving professional assignments to women in order to fulfill affirmative action programs; also, universities with declining enrollments no longer have a steady supply of student spouses to work in offices and libraries. As a result, many clerical jobs are being designed to allow for the constant turnover in personnel, and supervisors are hiring people with borderline qualifications. With the increasing emphasis on hiring permanent employees from the local community, people with physical disabilities, and retaining employees with alcohol- or drug-related problems, many job descriptions and assignments must be reevaluated and revised.

Family considerations often restrict people to a specific geographical area. The question of hiring people who hold master's degrees in library science as clerical staff is one of interest to many libraries.[29] The supervisor of such individuals is responsible for providing them with meaningful work without exploiting their advanced skills at a low salary. Also, requiring a degree from an ALA-accredited institution for professional staff bars from library employment available persons with degrees in media science or other related fields.

Student and other part-time employees are utilized in many types of libraries. They are often eligible for minimum wage. The employment of both full- and part-time employees is sometimes complicated when salaries are subsidized by nonlibrary funds, such as grants, work-study programs or CETA. If these funds expire, affected employees must be transferred to the library payroll or the services they performed must be eliminated.

Occupational Safety and Health

Another outside force affecting personnel is the federal Occupational Safety and Health Act.[30] Although universities are exempt from this federal law, some states have similar laws which apply to state agencies. Under current OSHA legislation, an employee dissatisfied with action taken on any complaint can report the incident to the state agency.

Motivation and Staff Development

Much is written on the supervisor's responsibility to motivate, but little on proven methods of accomplishing it. The idea of participative management in libraries has attracted a great deal of attention.[31] Under this method, all staff members concerned discuss a problem and suggest possible solutions. There is some disagreement whether the group should actually make the decision or simply provide input to the supervisor who then makes the decision. Tarr suggests that decisions should be reached through committees.[32] Mason has presented some ideas in opposition and warns that much time can be expended on "making employees happy" without improving services to users.[33]

Another area of supervisory management on which little information has appeared is the supervisor's responsibility for career development of subordinates. A study by Edwards found that supervisors viewed the first year or two of a librarian's career as a closely supervised training period.[34] Others felt that the beginning librarian should be able to assume specific responsibilities on the "first day" of employment.[35] The Office for Library Personnel Resources of ALA currently has a project entitled "Minimum Qualifications for Librarians." However, the extent of the supervisor's responsibility for the employee's failure to perform acceptably is not clear.

Collective Bargaining

It is at the supervisory level that collective bargaining has the most impact. Union contracts are negotiated with an organization's top management. Supervisors are then responsible for the performance of daily work within the constraints of the contract. Depending on contract provisions, decisions of hiring, training, promotion, salary schedules and terminations may be removed from the domain of the immediate supervisor, thus reducing his or her authority. Also, questions concerning changes, vacation assignments and filling vacancies may have to be negotiated with the union steward rather than directly with employees.

Equal Employment Opportunity

It is only recently that the Equal Employment Opportunity (EEO) guidelines have been applied to universities and other groups which receive grant money or other federal funds. It is the library administration's responsibility to see that supervisory management personnel have the information they need to conform to the regulations, such as those concerning interviewing and hiring procedures.

WHAT SUPERVISORS DO

Since supervisory management positions in libraries require a complex mixture of subject expertise, supervisory responsibilities and professional activities, there can be no simple description of what supervisors do. In previous studies this author looked at middle managers in academic and public libraries.[36] A new study examines supervisors and middle managers in corporation libraries.[37] In 1970, the Illinois State Library sponsored a comprehensive study entitled "A Task Analysis of Library Jobs in the State of Illinois";[38] other studies on this subject include those conducted by Canelas on academic libraries,[39] Ricking on public libraries,[40] and Wiese on school library media systems.[41]

I have investigated the extent to which people employed for two or four years would reach consensus regarding fourteen specific responsibilities. Two hundred questionnaires were sent to graduates of the University of Illinois Graduate School of Library Science for the years 1974-76; 104 usable replies were received. Of the respondents, 55 percent were employed in academic libraries, 22 percent in public libraries, 8 percent in schools, and 17 percent in other types of libraries. These respondents represent a higher proportion of academic librarians and lower proportion of public and school librarians than was reported in the placement statistics for 1974-76.[42]

Shera said library research can be described as "breaking down open doors."[43] Much of the following material falls in this category. Involvement in collective bargaining has led some library administrations to prepare guidelines distinguishing the duties of professional and clerical supervisors. For example, a Purdue University administrative memorandum states that hiring, dismissing, evaluating, disciplining, and administering wages must be handled by a professional supervisor, while the clerical supervisor is responsible for directing the activities of a work group or unit, may participate in employee evaluation, and may hire students for the work unit.

The literature has accorded little attention to the difference in supervisory techniques according to type of work performed and number and type of employees. The appropriate method of supervision depends on such factors as: (1) whether departmental people have face-to-face contact with clientele, (2) number of hours the unit is open, (3) number and classification of employees in the unit, (4) educational background of employees, and (5) whether it is a multibranch system and/or multilocation system. For instance, changing the hours of operation from forty to ninety-three per week may require greater reliance on written procedures, policies and regulations. Delegation of tasks increases and each person must know his or her exact responsibilities. Evaluation becomes a problem because the supervisor is not always present; he or she must observe job performance without seeming to spy or making informants of fellow employees.

In response to the author's survey, 98 percent of the respondents agreed that a supervisor evaluates the performance of employees, and 95 percent that the supervisor oversees the training of employees (see Table 1). Ninety-four percent agreed that supervisors recommend employees for discharge, and 91 percent indicated that they were responsible for overseeing work scheduling and recommending employees for promotion. Ninety percent agreed that supervisors must have detailed knowledge of the work performed in the unit, oversee the writing of job descriptions, and discipline employees.

TABLE 1. ATTITUDES OF LIBRARY SCHOOL GRADUATES TOWARD
SUPERVISORY RESPONSIBILITIES

Responsibilities of Supervisors	Percentage in Agreement
Evaluate employee performance	98.1
Oversee employee training	95.2
Recommend employee discharge	94.2
Oversee work scheduling	91.3
Recommend employee promotions	91.3
Have detailed knowledge of work performed in unit	90.4
Oversee writing of job descriptions of subordinates	90.4
Discipline employees	90.4
Decide how work should be performed in conjunction with employees	87.5
Have knowledge of conducting interviews to fill vacancies	87.4
Provide procedures manual	82.7
Have knowledge of grievance-handling	78.8
Have knowledge of EEO guidelines	74.0
Have knowledge of OSHA regulations	62.5

It is interesting to note that only 87 percent of the respondents felt that a supervisor should know how to conduct an interview to fill a vacancy. Since employee selection and evaluation are perhaps a supervisor's most important tasks, it seems that this should have been ranked higher. However, most employees are perhaps selected by department heads and assistant directors rather than by supervisors. Only 82 percent of the respondents believed supervisors should provide procedure manuals with detailed instructions on how to perform tasks; in industrial settings, instructing employees is one of the most frequently performed supervisory tasks.[44] That only 78 percent of the respondents recognized the handling of grievances as a supervisory responsibility is probably due to the fact that this is a local responsibility primarily involving libraries engaged in collective bargaining or those whose employees belong to unions.

Although ALA and other professional groups have been quite active in dispensing information about equal opportunity in employment, only 74 percent of the respondents viewed this knowledge as a responsibility of the supervisor. It is probably in the area of interviewing, selection, promotion, transfer and discharge — all areas of concern to supervisors — that most EEO violations occur.

The least amount of agreement among respondents concerned the area of occupational health and safety regulations. In interviewing middle managers and administrators two years ago, I found little concern about this topic. Safety receives a great deal of attention in the industrial setting. Most texts on supervision contain at least one chapter on the safety responsibilities of the industrial supervisor, and a recent thesis lists seventy-four such responsibilities.[45] Many unions are adding health and environmental specialists to their staffs to assist in evaluating working conditions. Although the library may not itself be governed by these or similar regulations, branch libraries located in departmental buildings where research is conducted may be affected. The regulations on providing access for the handicapped to all buildings require new layouts and designs for libraries. Most libraries housed in older buildings may discover potential safety hazards in flammable building materials, inaccessible nooks and crannies, improperly anchored shelving, overcrowded shelves, etc. Purely from the standpoint of human relations, library administrators should be concerned about safety precautions.

CONCLUSION

This overview of supervisory management has surveyed the library environment, the management "style" of the library, the demands for professionalism, and concern for employees. The trend is toward increased emphasis on personnel practices, especially those involving equal opportunity for employment, collective bargaining, occupational safety and health, and affirmative action.

REFERENCES

1. Heyel, Carl, ed. "Management Levels: Definitions," *The Encyclopedia of Management.* 2d ed. New York, Van Nostrand Reinhold, 1973, p. 503; and Gamaluddin, Ahmad F. "Decision-making at the Level of Middle Management: A Survey of Medium Sized Public Libraries." Ph.D. thesis, University of Pittsburgh, 1973, p. 66.

2. Dee, Joan M. "The Managerial Mystique: Obstacle or Opportunity?" Arlington, Va., ERIC Reproduction Service, 1977. (ED 149 457)

3. Fry, Bernard M., and White, Herbert S. *Publishers and Libraries: A Study of Scholarly and Research Journals.* Lexington, Mass., Lexington Books, 1976, pp. 19-28.

4. "Public Library Spending Still Climbing," *American Libraries* 9:483, Sept. 1978.

5. Morrison, Perry D. *The Career of the Academic Librarian* (ACRL Monograph No. 29). Chicago, ALA, 1969, pp. 83, 86; and Finks, Lee W. "Measuring the Attitudes of Library School Students Toward Intellectual Freedom, Innovation and Change, Service, Research and Administration and Management." Ph.D. thesis, Rutgers University, 1973.

6. Berry, John N. "Reporting the 'Bad News,' " *Library Journal* 103:915, May 1, 1978.

7. *See, for example,* "Georgia University Ousts Its Director," *Library Journal* 103:921-22, May 1, 1978.

8. Terkel, Studs. *Working.* New York, Pantheon, 1974; and Schrank, Robert. *Ten Thousand Working Days.* Cambridge, Mass., MIT Press, 1978.

9. Bailey, Martha J. *The Special Librarian as a Supervisor or Middle Manager* (State-of-the-Art Review No. 6). New York, Special Libraries Association, 1977.

10. Echelman, Shirley. "Libraries Are Businesses, Too!" *Special Libraries* 65:409-14, Oct./Nov. 1974.

11. Bailey, op. cit., pp. 5-15.

12. Minor, Barbara B., ed. "Proceedings of the Information Broker/Free Lance Librarian — New Careers — New Library Services Workshop Held at Drumlins, Syracuse, New York" (Miscellaneous Studies No. 3). Syracuse, N.Y., Syracuse University School of Information Studies, Aug. 1976.

13. Reynolds, Maryan E. "Challenges of Modern Network Development," *Journal of Academic Librarianship* 1:19-22, May 1975.

14. Parker, Thomas F. "Models and Methods: The Tools of Library Networking," *College & Research Libraries* 36:482, Nov. 1975.

15. *See* Booz, Allen and Hamilton, Inc. *Organization and Staffing of the Libraries of Columbia University: A Summary of the Case Study.* Westport, Conn., Redgrave Information Resources, 1973; and Webster, Duane E. "The Management Review and Analysis Program: An Assisted Self-Study to Secure Constructive Change in the Management of Research Libraries," *College & Research Libraries* 35:114-25, March 1974.

16. Heinritz, Fred J. "Modern Scientific Management in the Academic Library," *Journal of Academic Librarianship* 1:20, July 1975.

17. Parker, op. cit., pp. 480-86.

18. Petit, Thomas A. *Fundamentals of Management Coordination: Supervisors, Middle Managers, and Executives.* New York, John Wiley & Sons, 1975, p. 237.

19. Jackson, Ruth L. "Origin and Development of Selected Personnel Management Functions in the Field of American Librarianship, 1876-1969." Ph.D. thesis, Indiana University, 1976.

20. " 'Insubordination' Issue Taken Up by Calif. SRRT," *Library Journal* 100:1280-81, July 1975.

21. Binder, Michael B. "The Supervisory Behavior of Academic Library Cataloging and Processing Personnel: An Inquiry into Relationships with Certain Situational Factors." Ph.D. thesis, University of Pittsburgh, 1973, p. 80.

22. Gamaluddin, op. cit., p. 145.

23. Kay, Emanuel. *The Crisis in Middle Management.* New York, AMACOM, 1974, pp. 10, 13-19, 127, 143.

24. Gavryck, Jacquelyn A. "The SUNY Librarians' Faculty Status Game," *Journal of Academic Librarianship* 1:11-13, July 1975.

25. Tallau, Adeline, and Beede, Benjamin R. "Faculty Status and Library Governance," *Library Journal* 99:1521-23, June 1, 1974.

26. Bailey, Martha J. "Some Effects of Faculty Status on Supervision in Academic Libraries," *College & Research Libraries* 37:48-52, Jan. 1976.

27. "New Career 'Ladders' Pose Status Threat to Librarians," *Library Journal* 99:1746, July 1974; and Huston, Esther. " 'Alternate' Career Ladders" (letter to the editor), *Library Journal* 99:2558, Oct. 15, 1974.

28. Nollen, Stanley D., and Martin, Virginia H. *Alternative Work Schedules; Part I: Flexitime.* New York, AMACOM, 1978.

29. Dagnese, Joseph, ed. "The Employment of Professionals in Support Positions: A Symposium," *Journal of Academic Librarianship* 3:320-27, Jan. 1978.

30. See Eckles, Robert W., et al. "Safety and Health Responsibilities Under OSHA." In *Essentials of Management for First-Line Supervision.* New York, John Wiley & Sons, 1974, pp. 542-72; and Locke, John H. "Provision of Information and Advice for the Protection of Health and Safety at Work," *Aslib Proceedings* 28:8-16, Jan. 1976.

31. Marchant, Maurice P. *Participative Management in Academic Libraries.* Westport, Conn., Greenwood Press, 1976.

32. Tarr, Susan A. "Effective Group Process for Libraries: A Focus on Committees," *College & Research Libraries* 35:444-52, Nov. 1974.

33. Mason, Ellsworth. "Decisions! Decisions!" *Journal of Academic Librarianship* 1:4-8, March 1975.

34. Edwards, Ralph M. *The Role of the Beginning Librarian in University Libraries* (ACRL Publications in Librarianship, no. 37). Chicago, ALA, 1975.

35. "Californians Peg Entry Level Librarian I 'Tasks,' " *Library Journal* 102:2298-300, Nov. 15, 1977.

36. Bailey, Martha J. "The Position of the Middle Manager in the Academic Library Organization; Report on Council on Library Resources Fellowship 1975-76." West Lafayette, Ind., Purdue University, Physics Library, Sept. 1976. (ED 129 327); and _____. "The Qualifications of Middle Managers in Public Libraries." (In process.)

37. _____. "Middle and Supervisory Management in Corporation Libraries." (In process.)

38. "A Task Analysis of Library Jobs in the State of Illinois." Silver Springs, Md., Social and Educational Research and Development, Inc., May 1970. (ED 040 723)

39. Canelas, Dale B. "Task Analysis of Library Jobs in the State of Illinois: A Working Paper on the Relevance of the Study to Academic Libraries." Arlington, Va., ERIC Reproduction Service, Sept. 1971. (ED 067 113)

40. Ricking, Myrl. "Illinois Task Analysis Project: Phase II, A Study." Arlington, Va., ERIC Reproduction Service, Sept. 1971. (ED 067 111) *See also* _____, and Booth, Robert E. *Personnel Utilization in Libraries: A Systems Approach.* Chicago, ALA and Illinois State Library, 1974.

41. Wiese, Bernice M. "Proposals for an Organization Model, Job Descriptions, and Training Programs for the Supporting Staff of School Library Media Systems." Arlington, Va., ERIC Reproduction Service, 1971. (ED 067 112)

42. Learmont, Carol L., and Darling, Richard L. "Placements and Salaries 1976: A Year of Adjustment," *Library Journal* 102:1345-51, June 15, 1977; ————. "Placements and Salaries 1975: A Difficult Year," *Library Journal* 101:1487-93, July 1976; and Frarey, Carlyle J., and Learmont, Carol L. "Placements and Salaries 1974: Promise or Illusion?" *Library Journal* 100:1767-74, Oct. 1, 1975.

43. Shera, Jesse H. "Failure and Success: Assessing a Century," *Library Journal* 101:284, Jan. 1, 1976.

44. Sartain, Aaron Q., and Baker, Alton W. *The Supervisor and His Job.* 2d ed. New York, McGraw-Hill, 1972.

45. Goberni, Joseph M. "Safety Program Responsibilities of Supervisory Personnel." Ph.D. thesis, West Virginia University, 1977.

DONALD J. SAGER
Director
Public Library of Columbus and Franklin County
Columbus, Ohio

Leadership and Employee Motivation

While most people have a fair idea of what leadership is, there is some disagreement about the meaning of motivation. For many, motivation is the method used to get people to work. For others it represents higher salaries, fringe benefits and improved working conditions. Still others view it as a management exercise. By the end of this paper, I hope readers will have some different views of motivation and its implications for library supervisors.

It is appropriate to begin with a discussion of leadership, since it is essential to an understanding of motivation. Peter Drucker said that leadership is that quality of examining work to ensure that effort is not placed where there are no results. According to this definition, leadership is the skill of establishing priorities and marshalling resources to achieve worthwhile goals. While some may disagree with this definition, few will argue that Drucker's view is unreasonable. Supervisors have the difficult and primary task of determining what is important in their organization. Drucker advises them to forget about yesterday's services, to maintain today's breadwinners and, as managers, to emphasize and nurture tomorrow's objectives. Indeed, a fundamental rule of leadership is to delegate yesterday and undertake tomorrow. Those expensive experiences in management ego, in developing and maintaining services and collections long after analyses have revealed their failure, must be avoided. Leadership is the art of recognizing the mistake, even one's own, and correcting it before it bleeds the institution.

The leader is also the person who must ask himself and the members of his administrative team to redefine regularly the purpose and role of their institution. The leader must clarify the institution's goals and objectives and remind his team of those ends. To be successful, the leader must ensure that the team knows both the goals and the strategy.

This definition of leadership depicts the leader as a team player. Single all-powerful executives who make unilateral decisions affecting thousands of people are rarely heard of today. The task of management has become too complicated to permit such autonomy. This is especially true in library management, where the director's major role is to serve as an interface between governance, staff and clientele. Except in the smallest library, he rarely has the time or skill to direct all phases of the library's operation. The chief executive must delegate those responsibilities to others.

Today's leader must exercise a new type of skill, i.e., motivating people to achieve increasingly complex and costly goals. In the public sector that role is complicated by the limitations placed upon us of economics, legal and regulatory requirements, technology, and society. Nonetheless, just as any craftsman employs his tools to complete his work, so are leaders bound to employ human resources to achieve their goals.

In fulfilling managerial responsibilities, most of us are old enough to recognize that people are no longer willing to work as they once did. This is not necessarily either good or bad. Cheap and willing labor is no longer available in this country. Even student labor, so plentiful in the past, is becoming more difficult to obtain, and most students are unwilling to submit to the endless, mindless drudgery of shelving thousands of books. They will work, but prefer to do so in areas where they can gain useful experience which will further their own careers. To compete, libraries will have to devote more attention in the future to developmental programs which will give the person performing routine tasks a greater sense of responsibility. An advertisement in today's newspaper is no guarantee of getting a competent and willing worker for the salary you feel is competitive. Too often the solution seems to be a higher salary, but this is not necessarily so.

The worker of today is far different from that of twenty years ago. He is probably better educated. More than likely there are two breadwinners in the family. Women no longer see life and career in terms of their husbands; men are no longer the lords and masters of their households. The family continuity binding a worker to the same career his father had has ceased to exist. Very few workers today worry about securing themselves for their old age. We are a world of pleasure-seekers and only the masochist enjoys spending extra hours chained to his desk. We take the vacations, health insurance, sick leave and other fringe benefits for granted today; even salary has lost its luster. The ultimate fear of job loss has been cushioned by assurance of unemployment insurance, workmen's compensation, Equal Employment Opportunity, unions, due process, and social security. It makes no difference that it wasn't always so. All of this has become part of the employee's rights. The worker has indeed changed — and not necessarily for the worse. He has found dignity and pride, and those elements are the key to motivation in today's society.

A good understanding of the worker is necessary for an understanding of motivation. Traditionally, the prevailing definition of the worker has been inspired by the dominant institution in society. During the Middle Ages that institution was the Catholic church, which held forth the spiritual man and woman with the fundamental goal of salvation. From the eighteenth through the early twentieth centuries, the predominant institution was industry, from which sprang economic man and woman with the acceptable goal of making money. Today the prevailing definition is more difficult to identify, for 500 years of change have been concentrated into the last 25 years.

Frederick Taylor has been called the father of scientific management. He developed time-and-motion studies as a basic tool of management. He also proposed the concept of the worker as an interchangeable part, a role Taylor genuinely believed the worker preferred in that it relieved him of decision-making. Thus, mechanistic man and woman appeared and an era began which culminated with the Hawthorne studies.

The Hawthorne studies revealed that physical variables such as lighting and temperature do not affect production. Workers are more affected by other workers. Thus, the concept of social man and woman was proposed, and the human relations movement started. No sooner was this model accepted as a basis for motivating employees than it was discovered that workers were willing to restrict their individual output in order to earn the acceptance of their coworkers. Counseling was then initiated, and the emotional man and woman were created.

The relevance of this history to a discussion of motivation is that most supervisors took on their responsibilities during a period when one or several of these philosophies were in their ascendancy. Many continue to use the skills and techniques which applied to those times in today's entirely different environment.

There are currently as many different definitions of the American worker as there are management specialists. Frederick Herzberg has defined two varieties: the neo-mechanistic or instrumental man or woman, a detached specialist in today's computerized society; and the consumer, whose goal is immediate consumption — a quantum step away from the economic model of less than fifty or sixty years ago. The families seen wandering aimlessly through discount stores on Sunday afternoons, wondering where to spend their money first, are examples of the consumer model.

Whatever definition of the modern American worker is used, it is important to understand his goals in order to motivate him. People's goals vary, as Herzberg's two other definitions of the worker illustrate. Based on archetypes which he borrowed from the Old Testament, Herzberg saw the worker as represented by Adam and Abraham. Adam is an instinctively lazy man, only somewhat removed from the animal in that he is capable of perceiving an infinite variety of pain. Indeed, Adam perceives pain in three dimensions — past, present and future. He remembers pain, feels present pain, and anticipates future pain. The worker as Adam prevails because of this characteristic. He seeks to avoid pain by obtaining security, safety, good working conditions, salary and fringe benefits. Herzberg called these elements hygiene factors. They are essential to the animal in man and for some, they provide a powerful motivator. Abraham, however, is unique in Biblical experience. He entered into a covenant, or contract, with God which stated that certain things belong to God and certain things are reserved for Abraham. Abraham is a human being who strives for growth. He takes hygiene factors for granted; he is motivated by other goals.

As I noted, it is essential to determine what an individual likes or needs in his work if motivation is to occur. If people are asked what they want from their work, they will respond with many generalizations. In the library field, people are likely to say they like working with books or with other people. Until recently (before passage of California's Proposition 13), some librarians may have said that they liked their work because it was secure and had status. Others may say they like creating order out of chaos. However, if specific information is required, they must be asked to relate actual experiences, both good and bad. Studies performed on this basis show that people like the following aspects of their work, ranked in order of preference:

1. Achievement, a sense of being able to see something tangible derived from their effort, such as a well-organized collection or a new physical facility.
2. Recognition or appreciation from their supervisors or colleagues.
3. The work itself. A person who enjoys meeting people, for example, will have a greater interest in public service work than one who does not.
4. Increased responsibility, such as enlarging the job to reflect the individual's capabilities.
5. Advancement or promotion within the organization.
6. Opportunity to learn new things, or growth.

These same studies have also revealed the things people do not like about their jobs:

1. Restrictive policies or a restrictive administration. For example, if a librarian in public services finds that he is prevented from extending certain services or resources to patrons, he will become increasingly frustrated with his job.
2. Poor supervision. The manager who is unsupportive or incompetent is going to make life miserable for subordinates.
3. Poor interpersonal relationships. Unless an employee likes the people he works with, the job will clearly become undesirable.
4. Poor working conditions. If the environment is noisy, the lighting poor, or the temperature uncomfortable, these factors will obviously affect the way employees feel about their job.
5. Poor salary. Strange as it may seem, this is not the number one complaint. Salary is still important, but in the sense that an employee's belief that he is poorly paid can seriously affect his job performance.
6. Low status and lack of security.

From these results it is obvious that what makes people happiest and motivates them in their job is what they do. What makes them unhappiest is the situation in which they do it.

Returning to Herzberg's archetypes of Adam and Abraham, it can be seen that hygiene factors are related to job environment. To satisfy Adam, these factors must be dealt with. However, to satisfy Abraham, motivation or growth factors must be offered. In order to motivate someone, two things must be known. Is the individual satisfied with the hygiene factors offered by the job, i.e., salary, fringe benefits, security and status, and interpersonal relationships? Second, will the individual be challenged by the job?

Unfortunately, the latter factor is not easy to determine. I recall being interviewed once about the attribute I found most essential in the library profession. I told the reporter that I valued creativity more than any other. I could forgive any fault but its absence. When the reporter asked why I felt it was more valuable than technical competence or reliability, I responded that a truly creative person is self-motivating. All he needs is technical help, feedback and a little orientation about the institution's goals. In short, with a creative person there is no problem with providing motivation. Finding such workers, however, is another matter.

Managing the self-motivated person is an art. It is possible to frustrate and lose a valuable asset through overmanagement. Some managers believe that to motivate these persons a goal must be established that they cannot reach. However, people with high achievement motivation are already performing at their maximum. To be effective in managing the high achiever, stay out of his way. When I review the process of personnel evaluation with my staff, I often find those who feel it is redundant to evaluate the work of an effective, long-term employee. They consider evaluation appropriate only for the new or problem employee. Yet the self-motivated person needs the evaluation just as much. He requires reassurance and feedback about the effectiveness of his work. This is a form of recognition which makes his job worthwhile.

It is also important to realize that high achievers do not necessarily make good managers. There are different qualities involved, and all too often the motivation of high achievers can be destroyed by the assumption that they can translate those skills which made them successful in one aspect of the organization to another. That may not necessarily be the case. The familiar Peter Principle, which claims that an individual rises to his maximum level of incompetence, is too true to be humorous.

Another point to remember is that people have ideas of their own. If an individual is not allowed to exercise his creativity and initiative, he will surely be frustrated. This applies to everyone, not just the high achiever. While not everyone elects to exercise that right all the time, managers should not get into the habit of directing personnel in certain functions, or in ways that will kill initiative. I learned a technique from McDonald's sophisticated personnel training program which I think is pertinent. I once retained one of their regional training managers to explain some of their techniques to our first-line supervisors. He told us that to train a new employee, the supervisor should first go through the procedure to be learned, explaining and demonstrating to the employee how each step should be performed. Then the employee repeats the instructions while the instructor performs the steps. If the employee omits or confuses a step, the instructor does not stop to correct him, but simply continues following the incorrect instructions so the employee can witness the consequences. The last step of the training process requires the employee to demonstrate his mastery by performing the task for the supervisor.

The critical step is the middle one, in which the employee describes what is logical in his mind. Trainers continually learn that their way is not always the best way. Even a beginner can teach them how to do it better. McDonald's doesn't insist on one standard procedure if someone has a more effective way.

To understand employees, supervisors must attempt to look at the employees' work in the same way they do. I find that I continually have to relearn even the simplest functions because of what I observe in my staff. Supervisors have the grand concept that the world is perfectible.

Most employees know better and design their work routines in the face of hard realities, attempting to make the work more interesting, challenging and comfortable. This does not imply that supervisors should ignore their responsibility to initiate change and develop standard procedures. Without these actions, organizations stagnate and training cannot be effectively achieved. It does mean that management must recognize that the ultimate impact it has upon the client is not accomplished by the changes, policies or procedures it proposes, but rather by how the person at the front desk implements those proposals.

I believe that encouraging creative change is the ultimate motivator, provided that the changes are desirable and not implemented for their own sake. Innovation can make even a routine task important, for it gives the individual an opportunity to make a significant contribution through testing and implementing changes. The individual grows in the job, achieves a tangible goal, and should receive some recognition for the effort. These three things — growth, achievement and recognition — are elements which make people like their jobs.

Another theory of motivation — theory X and Y, developed by Douglas McGregor — has some important contributions to this review. When McGregor developed these terms he was seeking labels that would be as neutral as possible in order to avoid an implied preference for one theory over the other. In theory X management, the worker is conceived of as passive and inert, the lazy animal or Adam archetype discussed previously. Theory Y management depicts the worker as perfectible, as an individual with a need to grow. McGregor proposed that theory Y management does not imply letting people "do their own thing." He felt that management had an obligation to provide goals which were not only clear but determined collectively. At the same time, he did not wish to label theory X management as autocratic. The emphasis is on achieving harmony with discipline, McGregor explained; however, some people respond only to authority and do not wish to participate in decision-making.

McGregor's contribution to the study of motivation underlined the importance of flexibility: application of theory X or Y management techniques should depend on the individual being supervised and the circumstances. I learned much about management techniques when I worked for General Motors many years ago. GM experimented, as did many other corporations, with a matrix organizational structure in contrast to a traditional hierarchy. When I entered public service and directed my own library, I believed that this structure might be relevant to the library profession, with public service functions placed along one axis of the grid and supportive functions along the other. I finally came to the realization that it would not work. Although the library possesses a professional atmosphere, many of the employees simply resisted participation in decision-making. They were interested in certain aspects of their job and were satisfied to remain there. Participation in the management of the institution caused a great deal of insecurity feelings among them, and friction and indecision resulted. Rather than adopt a uniformly participative management style, a supervisor must adjust his management approach according to the character and motivation of the individuals on his administrative staff. Although the library profession currently tends to stress theory Y, there are tasks which do not permit much flexibility. When assigning those tasks that do, however, the assignment should include a major responsibility in determining how the problem should be attacked, provided the person wishes to have that involvement. People need to have a stake in their work; they do not want things done to them. For many managers this involves a degree of risk, for often it is their job and reputation that is in jeopardy if their staff fails. This necessitates careful definition of the problem: identification of supervisory responsibility and staff responsibility. Nonetheless, supervisors must be willing to take such risks in order to motivate their staffs. Supervisors can neither run their organization by fear nor fear to run it; rather, they must walk the line between these extremes.

Another significant contributor to the study of motivation is Chris Argyris, who was concerned with the phenomenon of built-in obsolescence. Argyris's work dealt primarily with the problem of repetitive tasks in industry. Motivation under these circumstances was found to be extremely difficult. Most assembly-line workers had resigned themselves to the fact that there was no future or inherent interest in their jobs. The only motivation their supervisors could offer was higher wages. However, Argyris realized that the cost of motivating alienated people is very high. To deal with this problem, Argyris concentrated on granting more responsibility to each worker, often assigning full responsibility for assembling entire units rather than single sections. He found that production usually dropped temporarily but soon picked up, along with employee motivation and morale. He demonstrated that the price management pays for poor motivation is poor morale and, eventually, higher costs.

The greater lesson Argyris taught is that people need feedback about their impact on the organization. If they lack pride and respect for their roles in the organization, their energies will be directed elsewhere. In some institutions, "beating the system" is an employee's most creative activity. If employees are treated as nothing more than warm bodies, that is all they will be. If institutions are to avoid the resulting obsolescence, they must stop the mistrust which seems to permeate them, seeping down from the upper levels of management to the public service desk.

Clearly, some tasks cannot be made more interesting or challenging. These jobs, all too common in the library field, are the ones which should be automated out of existence. Library work is one of the most labor-intensive services in the public sector, and each feasible opportunity to automate ought to be embraced. Where this is not possible, workers should not be insulted by attempts to convince them that they should be happy in performing that task.

Certain techniques are commonly employed in attempting to motivate persons performing these tasks, but they have not been very effective. For example, job rotation has often been suggested to help workers cope with repetitive tasks. However, this is not a solution; it only provides workers with varieties of pain. A switch from washing dishes to washing silverware still means you're washing eating utensils — a necessary task only if an automatic dishwasher is not available. However, it is possible to enlarge such tasks as Argyris did in his assembly-line experiments. Giving additional responsibility to an individual can enrich his job and provide greater motivation.

Retraining is often recommended for employees who have become obsolete in their jobs; it has the dual function of making the individual more productive for the institution and of motivating him through an awareness of the investment the institution has made in him. This is not an uncommon problem in librarianship, due to increasing automation in the field. However, resurrection is much more difficult than giving birth; it is far better to prevent obsolescence by making certain that each job keeps people up to date.

A sound basis for motivation in any library is an adequate budget for staff development. A reasonable figure is 2 percent of the personnel budget, which is the amount the more progressive industries allocate. I suspect that few libraries spend more than a fraction of this on staff development. Our record in this area is no better than that of many other professions, despite our alleged role in society of promoting continuing education. We think nothing of placing someone with twenty years of experience on the shelf in order to hire a recent graduate familiar with new technology and resources. Unfortunately, society is becoming educated more to do less, and the result is frustration and a vast underutilization of talent.

Douglas McGregor made the classic statement that each person should be approached with an open mind and not an open mouth. Each person must be allowed to demonstrate his ability. If employees cannot demonstrate sufficient competence or willingness to correct professional deficiencies, then replacement may be considered. Often the challenge of new responsibilities which are a result of technological or social change affecting the organization will serve as motivation to produce a truly effective employee.

Motivation has always been a worldwide problem. People have tried to get others to do something by asking them, by applying psychology, by assigning through various communication techniques, by offering money, and by training. The most common motivational technique, however, has probably been the use of threat. Frederick Herzberg calls this KITA (kick in the "pants"), or negative physical means. Being somewhat more humane today, we generally resort only to strong language or one-upmanship. (Besides, today's individual would be likely to kick back.) Whether verbal or physical KITA is used, the result is the same: either the employee performs a specified task, or he is threatened with loss of his job.

KITA is movement, not motivation. Even society's elaborate reward system is simply positive KITA. Better salaries, fringe benefits, better communications and all the other various human relations trappings are like dog biscuits tossed out by managers to any employee performing the desired task.

A truly motivated person does a good job because it's important to him and to the institution. Motivation does not consist of threats or benefits, but of the ideas, feelings and attitudes an employee has about his job. In order to motivate your employees, you must ensure that they are correctly placed, challenged and involved in the determination of how their respective tasks are to be accomplished.

I don't mean to imply that salary, fringe benefits, good working conditions and security are not important, but they are only factors which, if present, will help to avoid dissatisfaction. By themselves they rarely motivate. If they are inadequate, however, it will be difficult to motivate anyone.

In summation, for motivation to be successful, people who are qualified and interested in the task should be selected — not the overqualified or those incapable of growing with the job as it evolves. If you are fortunate enough to recruit a creative, self-motivated person, don't frustrate that person through overmanagement. The self-motivated are already performing at their maximum. Get out of their way. Help them with feedback and technical assistance, and orient them to the goals of the organization. Broaden the abilities of those who are not self-motivated by aiding them to establish challenging goals. Do not prescribe those goals; rather, provide general guidance and let the individual determine the specifics. Allow people to participate in decisions affecting them, and let yourself be influenced by their recommendations. Don't neglect the hygiene factors (salary, fringe benefits, etc.); no matter how much food you may eat now, you will get hungry again. Automate the repetitive jobs whenever possible. If you cannot do so, then seek to motivate the persons performing those tasks by enlarging their jobs and giving them more responsibility. Don't be afraid to take risks with people. Consider the role of change and innovation in your organization: if a change is desirable and people are involved in its testing and implementation, it can itself serve as a powerful motivator.

Finally, remember that what really motivates people and makes them happy is what they do. What makes them unhappy and turns them against their job is the situation in which they do it.

SOURCE

Information for this paper was drawn from a series of management videotapes available from Advanced Systems, Inc. (1601 Tonne Rd., Elk Grove Village, Ill. 60007). Pertinent titles in this series are:

Managing Time from the "Effective Executive Series," with Peter Drucker;
To Be Efficient and To Be Human from the "Motivation: Management for Success Series," with Frederick Herzberg;
Myths About Your Employees from the "Motivation: Management for Success Series," with Frederick Herzberg;
Theory X and Y from the "Motivation and Productivity Series," with Saul Gellerman; and
Management of Human Assets from the "Motivation and Productivity Series," with Saul Gellerman.

DAVID R. DOWELL
Assistant University Librarian for Personnel
Duke University
Durham, North Carolina

The Role of the Supervisor in Training and Developing Staff

My experience indicates that there are two key elements in getting work done through people. The first is to select the right person for each position and the second is to give each staff member the training needed to do the job well. I believe supervisors should be evaluated on and held accountable for the degree to which their units contribute to the achievement of organizational objectives. That is why, as a personnel director, I believe supervisors must be given the authority to initiate recommendations in the areas of staffing and training. They should be able to justify their recommendations of who they believe should be hired and of what training their staff members should receive. Thus, supervisors should in turn receive the training they need in order to make and justify these recommendations successfully.

My conviction that staffing and training are the two most important elements in successful supervision was, until recently, based only on intuitive feelings. Now, however, empirical data have been collected in support of this conclusion. Unfortunately, librarians seldom believe that studies conducted in industry have any relevance to libraries. The study I am about to describe, however, was conducted in the Rutgers University Library. In a 1976 dissertation, Alan Bare studied the relationship between the performance of forty-three work groups and the participation of the groups' supervisors in the following activities: (1) counseling and team building, (2) coordination and control, (3) staffing, (4) formalizing, (5) training, (6) external representation, (7) communication and feedback, and (8) performance-reward contingency management. Positive correlations at a level of significance too great to be attributed to chance were found to exist between group performance and four of these eight supervisory variables, i.e., staffing, training, performance-reward contingency management, and counseling and team building.

The supervisory activities with the most significant relation to group performance were staffing and training. These were related at the .01 confidence level, i.e., this relationship was so strong that it would randomly occur in less than one in one hundred cases. Bare measured the supervisors' staffing activities by examining the degree to which raters agreed or disagreed with the following statements:

s/he hires the most competent people available;
s/he hires people who fit well with job requirements;
s/he makes sure the group has the talents it needs;
s/he has good ideas;
s/he tries new ways of doing things; and
s/he defines jobs in a way that makes good use of the talents we have.[1]

Note that there may in fact be differences between the first and second of these statements. There are situations in which the most experienced, competent or best-educated person available is not the one who best fits the requirements of the job, or in which the most trainable candidate may have fewer of the qualifications required to succeed in a job than other candidates. In university libraries, even low-level clerical openings will attract applicants with a fairly high level of education. Often a choice must be made between a college graduate with a background in one or more foreign languages and a high school graduate with business and/or clerical training. Which is better qualified for a library clerical job? It is generally assumed that the better-educated and/or more intelligent candidate will learn the routines of the position more quickly and require less of the supervisor's time before reaching an acceptable level of independent performance. However, this person may become quickly bored and more readily turn to another employer offering a more challenging and/or better-paying position. A supervisor may have to train several of these "quick learners" for a single job over the same period of time needed to train one employee less easily bored with the work. However, there is no easy way to be certain beforehand, so whichever choice is made, the supervisor should be aware of the possible consequences.

In measuring a supervisor's training competency, Bare asked raters to indicate whether they agreed or disagreed with the following statements:

s/he provides opportunities to learn on the job;
s/he encourages participation in formal training programs;
s/he encourages self-development; and
s/he delegates challenging assignments.[2]

It is not hard to understand why the work units with supervisors highly rated in these areas were also the most productive. It is especially true in libraries that people are the most important resource. In most libraries, about two-thirds of the budget is spent on wages and benefits. Therefore, unless these human resources are well managed, there is little chance that patrons will receive their money's worth in services. Unless staff members have the knowledge and skills needed to perform their job responsibilities competently, they cannot be expected to contribute what is required for the library to reach its service objectives.

On the basis of both common sense and Bare's empirical data, it seems unquestionable that time spent in training and developing staff is time well spent. Yet, I still must question that assumption — even though it leads to a threefold conflict of personal interests. As a librarian, I have a strong belief in the value of education to society. As a member of the academic staff of an institution of higher learning, I have invested a portion of my life in contributing to the liberal arts background and professional training of its students. As the library staff development officer, I have a responsibility for the training and development of the library's entire staff. In spite of these commitments, I believe it is necessary to place some limitations on the training and development activities of supervisors.

Libraries do not exist to provide training and development for their staff members, but rather to provide services to their clients. Staff training and development should never become an end in itself. There is little reason to believe that the most trained and developed staff is the most productive staff *unless* there is a strong correlation between the areas of training and development and the areas of competence needed to perform work assignments. At least one study has shown that there was no apparent difference between the performance of engineers who took continuing education courses and those who did not.[3] Training should always provide the specific knowledge and/or skills needed to improve the ability of a staff member to perform a specific task in the most effective way. This training is the legitimate and necessary responsibility of every supervisor.

However, the training which makes the best use of human resources includes more than simply the knowledge necessary to perform a specific job. Orientation and training efforts must go beyond this. An old story will illustrate this point. Four workers performing identical duties were asked separately what they were doing. One replied, "I'm making ten dollars an hour." Another answered, "I'm laying bricks." A third stated, "I'm building a wall," while the fourth responded, "I'm helping to build a great cathedral."

Supervisors must be careful not always to take an employee's comments at face value, however. They may not really indicate the employee's actual level of understanding due to real or false humility or any number of other reasons. Certainly there are many times when a supervisor would be happy to settle for workers who understood that the task at hand was to lay bricks; it is therefore easy to appreciate how helpful it would be if workers understood that the individual bricks were to become a wall. It is the supervisor's role to see that employees understand how the quality and quantity of their personal efforts contribute to the success of the organization as a whole. If staff members are to view their work in this manner, it will be as a result of a well-conceived and well-executed plan. Such a plan involves matching the library's needs with the abilities of individual staff members. Two management consultants suggest the following strategy:

1. The tasks performed by each employee constitute outputs in goods and services that are explicitly related to achieving the recognized goals of the organization.
2. The majority of each employee's work time is actually devoted to performing these tasks.
3. The majority of each employee's time is spent working at his or her highest knowledge/skill level as perceived by both supervisor and employee.
4. The majority of employees are responding to a climate that encourages the expenditure of levels of energy and effort that are perceived as high by those both inside and outside the organization.
5. The workflow in most production or service units is structured to minimize both slack time and duplication of effort.
6. Formal and informal organizational structures are integrated with technology in a way that improves task performance.[4]

These conditions are likely to be achieved only if staff have learned to analyze their own performance and to adjust it as the occasion demands.

Once beyond training staff for a specific job, it is often difficult to know how far a staff development program can go and still be cost-effective. In making this determination it is useful to distinguish between staff development and continuing education.

Continuing education as a part of the concept of lifelong learning is clearly an idea whose time has come. The obsolescence of technical training has rapidly escalated in recent years, due to the greatly increased rate of change. This trend is likely to continue to accelerate. Some means must be found to help individuals continue to grow and develop. Whose responsibility is it to provide these opportunities for individuals?

Some staff members have no interest in personal development, while others have development interests that have very little to do with their jobs. As Edgar Schein recently pointed out: "Work and career are not as central a life preoccupation as was once the case. Perhaps because of a prolonged period of economic affluence, people see more options for themselves and are increasingly exercising those options. In particular, one sees more concern with a balanced life in which work, family, and self-development play a more equal role."[5] An extreme stereotype of this kind of person was illustrated in a 1975 Doonesbury cartoon in which Mark was having a conversation with his father:

Father: Son, have you given any thought to the sort of job you want when you graduate?
Mark: Oh, sure. I don't know what field it'll be in, but I know that it will have to be creative — a position of responsibility, but not one that restricts personal freedom. It must pay well. The atmosphere, relaxed, informal; my colleagues, interesting, mellow, and not too concerned with a structured working situation.
Father: In short, you have no intention of getting a job.
Mark: I didn't say that.

The concepts of staff development and continuing education have existed for a long time. However, they did not reach their current state of importance in libraries until the 1970s. As with most fads, the "pendulum effect" was operating: in the excitement of applying a new idea, society generally gets carried away, and swings from one extreme to the other. This physical science phenomenon is imitated by organizations every time a new idea is introduced. Too often new ideas are rejected without a fair hearing. However, once an idea is adopted, its advocates often go overboard in implementing it; it is expected to solve everyone's problems. No single idea or innovation is likely to satisfy this kind of expectation. The foray of libraries into the areas of staff development and continuing education has led toward a more complete use of the available human resources, but it has also contributed to some very unproductive use of staff time. Supervisors are only beginning to learn when concentrating on staff development may be beneficial to ultimate productivity and when it may be counterproductive to the delivery of services to patrons.

In learning to differentiate judiciously, it is important to remember the difference between staff development and continuing education. It is in the area of overlap of the developmental interests of the staff member and those competencies needed in the library that the most effective training and development takes place. The initial employment interview is the ideal time to begin to assess whether this overlap is sufficient to make training of that person worthwhile. In this process, it must be recognized that individuals have legitimate continuing education interests that do not coincide with the library's needs, and libraries require certain competencies that particular individuals have no interest and/or ability to develop. However, both these elements — the interest and ability to learn on the part of the individual, and the need of the library — must be present before training will result in successful staff development.

It is very important that the collective goal of the staff be similar to the stated goal of the library. If they are not, then neither goal is likely to be harmoniously satisfied. A brief examination of vectors may help illustrate this point (see Figure 1). Vectors are lines which represent the direction and intensity of certain forces. The longer the line, the more powerful the force. The direction and intensity of the management's efforts to achieve the library's stated goal affects the actual role the library plays in providing its services. However, the direction and intensity of staff members' efforts also have an effect and must be taken into account. It is the interaction of these forces that is most important. In a laboratory setting, the vector representing the result of this interaction would indicate the direction and intensity of the library's actual performance. This model from elementary physics can easily be applied to the goals of the supervisor and employees of a library to describe some very complex organizational behavior.

So much for theory; what most supervisors really want are practical suggestions that can be applied on the job. With that in mind, I suggest that the process of identifying training needs begin before initiating the recruitment process. Before even advertising a position opening, the supervisor should list the areas of competency that a fully functioning staff member is required to master for that position. Then the supervisor should decide which of these competencies can reasonably be learned in the context of the work environment. All other competencies should become minimum qualifications for that position, that is, pass/fail requirements that *must* be met before the candidate can be seriously considered. The competencies that could reasonably be gained on the job become desirable qualities to be sought in the candidates who have met the minimum qualifications. Theoretically, the best-qualified candidate is the one that has demonstrated all the minimum qualifications and offers more optional competencies than any other. Other factors, such as dem-

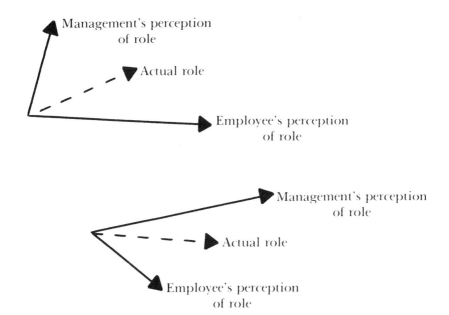

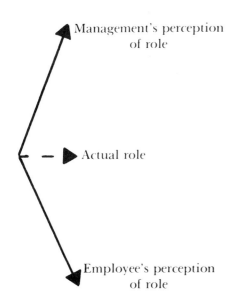

FIGURE 1. Vectors Illustrating How the Degree of Agreement Between Management and Employees Will Affect the Performance of an Organization.

onstrated learning ability, may also be a legitimate consideration. Once the selection decision is made, the training needs of the new staff member should be obvious *if* the above suggestion has been followed. The task of the supervisor is to provide the opportunity and assistance needed for the staff member to develop the additional competencies required for successful job performance, as well as to develop those competencies that were satisfactorily demonstrated when the hiring decision was made.

This process sounds much simpler than it actually is. However, thought and planning will save a lot of time and prevent wasted and counterproductive efforts later.

The actual training of a new staff member begins during the employment interview — if not before. During the interview the applicant is participating in an orientation to the interviewer as a supervisor, to the position available, possibly to other members of the work group, to the work area, to the library itself, and to the larger organization of which the library is a part. The session can lead to wise decisions on the part of the supervisor and applicant as to whether it is in their mutual interest to establish an employment relationship.

What kind of messages does the supervisor as interviewer send? Is the candidate treated with respect? Does the supervisor really listen to what the candidate says? Does the supervisor appear to know what is to be accomplished in the interview? Is the time effectively used in discussing job-related issues? Does the supervisor appear to know what the library, the job, the other employees, and the applicant are all about? What attitudes about them are being relayed? Is it made clear that the applicant will be expected to think if he or she becomes an employee? Tentative, if unconscious, impressions will be formed in all these areas. Without care, counterproductive learning may take place that will have to be "unlearned" if the candidate is to become a productive employee. In many ways, how the interview is conducted is at least as important as what is actually said.

This will be true of many other aspects of training. Fran Tarkenton recently related the following example of how actions speak louder than words:

> I was recently told by the vice-president of a major industrial firm that his superior, the executive vice-president, wanted him to be more creative. But, he recalled that every time he brought an idea that he thought was new and creative to the executive vice-president, he was told all the things that were wrong with the idea. The executive vice-president wants and is directing his managers to be more creative, yet punishes creativity. He is not likely to get, and certainly will not maintain, creative thinking and innovation in his organization.[6]

As supervisors you should try to recall the last time a subordinate or a peer offered an idea or a suggestion. Has it been a long time? What was your response? Would it encourage or discourage the person to volunteer an idea again? As Tarkenton put it, "People, not dollars, create."[7]

The reader is probably wondering why I am belaboring the apparently self-evident importance of staff training and development. The fact is, most supervisors do not give sufficient attention to this responsibility. This is not necessarily because they believe that training is unimportant. According to Samuel Phifer, Executive Training Director of Allied Stores Corporation, the reasons supervisors give this activity insufficient attention are subtle:

> They are afraid of surrendering vital information derived from experience. Holding on to this information gives them a feeling of being needed, a sense of personal power and control. Yielding information is seen as a weakening of this power. Another frequent reason for avoiding the responsibility to train is that supervisors do not know how to go about it and are not anxious to have that deficiency exposed. Still others feel that to train and develop subordinates properly, it would be expected that they know all the details of each of their jobs. To have this lack of knowledge revealed would also be an embarrassment. And, finally, there are supervisors who are not at all sure where to draw the line between managing and developing. They are unclear as to what constitutes training as distinguished from good communications, capable direction, and sound control and discipline.[8]

Although I have observed ample evidence to support each of Phifer's points, I believe he omitted the most prevalent reason library supervisors do not fulfill their training obligation. Many see themselves as workers first and supervisors second. They fail to realize that supervising is as much their responsibility as is the work of their unit. They feel guilty if they are not doing as much of the routine work as their subordinates. Therefore, little time and energy are left for uniquely supervisory activities.

No training should take place unless a specific need for it has been identified. This can be done in a number of ways. If the above suggestion is followed, some training needs will have been identified by the time an applicant is offered a position. In this case, the training needs are those competencies which are required and have yet to be developed. In other cases, employees may ask specifically for training to increase their ability to perform their jobs. It may be that an employee is observed as having difficulty performing his or her job due to inadequate knowledge or skills. Perhaps changes, such as the introduction of computers or the reorganization of workflow will require knowledge and skills not previously needed. However, as training needs manifest themselves, it is the supervisor's responsibility to recognize and act on them.

However an apparent need for training is recognized, the desired outcome is much more likely to be achieved if the supervisor can articulate to staff members exactly what new abilities the training will provide. Only then can the precise nature of the training be determined. The object during training is to minimize the disruption of current services while at the same time maximizing the potential of future services. This is no mean feat, but such is the nature of supervision.

One method of analyzing training needs is presented in a monograph by Robert Mager and Peter Pipe entitled *Analyzing Performance Problems, or "You Really Oughta Wanna."*[9] Mager and Pipe present a series of questions in a simple decision flow-chart. Working through the flow-chart to the solution involves a very useful thought process. However, as supervisors learn, solutions to many problems are not easily reached, and while no single method or technique will solve all problems, many of the ideas of others can be adapted to advantage.

Once a supervisor has clearly defined a training requirement, it must be decided who can best provide the needed training. Research indicates that training will be mastered more completely if two elements are included. First, if the trainee believes that the trainer controls the reward system, and the trainer actually has a high degree of control, more effective training will take place.[10] This finding indicates that the most effective training may be that provided by the supervisor if the supervisor is seen by the employee to be able to initiate recommendations for hiring, firing, promotions, salary increases and disciplinary action. Second, research also indicates that the trainee will learn more completely when the trainer is perceived to be competent in the task being taught.[11] This finding too may suggest that the supervisor is the most appropriate person to provide the needed instruction; on the other hand, it may suggest a better choice.

There are also criteria to consider when determining whether training should take place "on the job" or in a classroom setting. Martin Broadwell, author of *The Supervisor and On-the-Job Training*, uses a very practical and often entertaining handbook approach. Following is a summary of Broadwell's main points on the advantages and disadvantages of on-the-job training:[12]

Advantages of on-the-job training	Advantages of classroom training
Communication on a one-to-one basis	Fewer distractions
Can build on existing and ongoing relationships	More efficient use of trainer time
More natural setting (under actual work conditions)	Not all supervisors are good teachers
More efficient use of trainee time	Teaching technology is easier to apply
Less interference with production	

Whichever setting is used, appropriate training methods should be employed. There are a number of good books on this topic. Broadwell's book provides a practical, down-to-earth approach. Mager's *Preparing Instructional Objectives*[13] is also highly recommended. Two periodicals that provide practical help to first-line supervisors are *Supervision* and *Supervisory Management*.[14] Malcolm Knowles's classic *The Modern Practice of Adult Education*[15] is a very useful, substantive work. (If a supervisor does not have reason to believe a potential trainee can respond as an adult, perhaps that supervisor should be contemplating some other kind of personnel action.) No training method is appropriate in all settings, for all learning objectives, or for all trainees. Nor is one training method appropriate for all instructors. Rather, the method must be carefully chosen for the particular combination of circumstances.

Whatever method is employed, the results should be evaluated. Repeating failures with successive generations of workers must be avoided. Also, in the event that a training method is judged to have failed, an alternate method must be instituted. Evaluation will clarify whether the fault was with the training, or if the trainee is incapable of learning that particular skill or is simply not interested. Another possibility is that environmental factors may interfere with learning. Whatever the result of the training, if the need for it was sufficient to invest the time of the trainer and the trainee in the first place, it is worth knowing to what extent the original objective has been met.

The best way of evaluating whether the training has achieved its objective is to answer the question: Can the employees satisfactorily perform the task which they previously could not? The primary objective should not be to change attitudes; there is little convincing evidence that this type of training is effective. Moreover, attitudinal change is impossible to measure. Phifer suggests that "if we have trained well, we will have brought about a change in attitude as a consequence of our efforts."[16] Staff members who are confident that they have received the training and support they need to contribute productively to the library will have more positive attitudes than those who feel inadequate because of a lack of such preparation. The ultimate measure of a supervisor's success as a trainer and developer of staff is improved services to the library's patrons. As the 1980s approach, library costs are increasing faster than the general rate of inflation. Now, more than ever, patrons deserve the best service libraries can afford to provide.

REFERENCES

1. Bare, Alan C. "Staffing and Training: Neglected Supervisory Functions Related to Group Performance," *Personnel Psychology* 31:112, Spring 1978.
2. Ibid.
3. Dalton, Gene W., et al. "The Four Stages of Professional Careers — A New Look at Performance by Professionals," *Organizational Dynamics* 6:19-42, Summer 1977.
4. Giblin, Edward J., and Ornati, Oscar A. "Optimizing the Utilization of Human Resources," *Organizational Dynamics* 5:19, Autumn 1976.
5. Schein, Edgar H. "Increasing Organizational Effectiveness through Better Human Resource Planning and Development," *Sloan Management Review* 19:4, Fall 1977.
6. Tarkenton, Fran. "Encouraging Creativity," *Sky* 7:10, Oct. 1978.
7. Ibid.
8. Phifer, Samuel H. "Need for On-the-Job Training," *Supervision* 40:3, June 1978.
9. Mager, Robert F., and Pipe, Peter. *Analyzing Performance Problems, or "You Really Oughta Wanna."* Belmont, Calif., Fearon, 1970.
10. Justis, Robert T., et al. "The Effect of Position Power and Perceived Task Competence on Trainer Effectiveness: A Partial Utilization of Fiedler's Contingency Model of Leadership," *Personnel Psychology* 31:83-93, Spring 1978.
11. Ibid.
12. Broadwell, Martin. *The Supervisor and On-the-Job Training.* 2d ed. Reading, Mass., Addison-Wesley, 1975, pp. 29-34.
13. Mager, Robert F. *Preparing Instructional Objectives.* Palo Alto, Calif., Fearon, 1962.
14. *Supervision.* G.B. McKee, ed. National Research Bureau, 424 N. Third St., Burlington, Iowa 52601. 1939- ; and *Supervisory Management.* Ernest C. Miller, ed. American Management Associations, Trudeau Road, Saranac Lake, N.Y. 12983. 1955-
15. Knowles, Malcolm. *The Modern Practice of Adult Education; Andragogy vs. Pedagogy.* New York, Association Press, 1970.
16. Phifer, op. cit.

Making the Transition from Employee to Supervisor

In preparing the institute program, the planning committee decided to invite representative professional librarians who had recently experienced the role change from supervisee to supervisor (which frequently includes the responsibility of supervising former colleagues) to describe the experiences and problems they encountered in making this shift. Following is a summary of their observations.*

The first speaker was David Passmore, Head of the Cataloging Department at the University of Kansas Library. Before coming to the University of Kansas, he had served as a paraprofessional language/literature cataloger at the University of Iowa, and had had no previous administrative experience. He had been at the University of Kansas only a year when his department head requested a transfer, and a quick decision was made to replace him with Passmore. He now supervises a staff of eleven full-time professionals, approximately twenty full-time paraprofessionals, and three student assistants who work about ten to twelve hours a week. He described the feeling of being a supervisor as knowing that while one employee was making love to him, another was in the basement boiling tar and plucking feathers.

Passmore inherited many problems with the job. Among these was poor inter/intradepartmental communication. No clear chain of command existed and Passmore discovered that several units were doing the same thing. No one had established any standards. Most of the policies and

---

* Since the panel members' remarks were presented somewhat extemporaneously, rather than from formal papers, the summary of this session was prepared by Holly Wagner of the Graduate School of Library Science Publications Office.

procedures being used had never been written down. Rectifying this oversight was a difficult task, made even harder by the superimposition of OCLC on the existing poorly organized manual system. There was also a lot of infighting; the paraprofessionals (whom Passmore found to be dissatisfied and thus career-paranoid) especially were in disagreement with each other, their department head and other professionals.

There were problems that developed directly from Passmore's promotion as well. For instance, he found himself in the uncomfortable position of having to direct not only former colleagues but also his former supervisor. She was a woman with twenty-one years of library experience, a member of the "old guard." He preferred not to have to oppose her and instead tried to call upon her experience. Eventually they both adjusted to their changed professional relationship.

Administrative problems built into the job included complicated interdepartmental practices. For example, the civil service forms which the library was required to use were confusing. Passmore found cover notes on employee interview forms with personality characteristics such as "pleasant" and "crabby" written under *disposition,* i.e., whether or not the employee was hired. The library was also embroiled in an uncomfortable situation with civil service job reclassifications, a process which was to take two years and made a lot of people edgy.

Another shock resulted from Passmore's confrontation with his first annual faculty report assignment; he found that none had been written for the preceding year. He was suddenly responsible for setting goals and precedents after having been in the position only six months. Other headaches: 300,000 volumes in the library were unavailable because they had not been cataloged, and a newly-hired science librarian wanted permission to "clean up" the old files.

In an attempt to deal with these problem areas, Passmore instituted governance by committee. This system involved a lot of meetings and presented the difficulty of coordinating a large number of people. The final analysis was, however, that although it was hard, it was worthwhile and even fun.

The question of how to deal with employees who are having personal problems prompted Passmore to ask: What do employees do with a supervisor who has such problems? Recognizing that his own personal difficulties would make him unable to counsel his employees with similar problems, he openly informed his staff of his troubles and asked them to cooperate with him by understanding that he would judge whether he could help them or should defer assistance because of his own difficulties.

The second speaker, Tom Tomczak, Coordinator of General Materials and Services at the Milwaukee Public Library, explained first that General Materials and Services was not a subject catalog, but rather included materials such as serials, documents, microforms, maps, vertical files, and newspaper clippings, and services such as telephone and general reference service as well as interlibrary loan. Tomczak supervises a staff of nineteen full- and part-time employees, of whom nine are professionals, seven are paraprofessionals and three are clerical.

Tomczak was very familiar with the Milwaukee Public Library when he became a supervisor. Beginning as a library page, he has worked there for twenty years, taking time out for military service and to attend the University of Denver Graduate School of Librarianship. He described his promotion at the age of forty as a "midlife crisis": he felt he was abandoning his career in librarianship to become an administrator.

Tomczak now enjoys his change in position, however; he finds it brings both advantages and new problems. For instance, he is administratively over one of his first supervisors, and all the people in his department were once his peers. In his opinion, there are two errors that can be made in adjusting to supervising coworkers: to pretend that nothing has happened to change working relationships, or to attempt to establish distance. The first alternative is nonsense, and the second doesn't work either. Neither the staff nor the supervisor should lean on their former relationship for favors or in expectation of extra effort. The only solution is to allow relationships to regain their naturalness after a period of adjustment. As a result of this attitude, he does not perceive an excessive distance between himself and his staff, or believe that anyone is trying to take advantage of past relationships.

According to Tomczak, delegation of responsibility is the most important part of a supervisor's job. Even while working as a page, he had acquired some management experience and skills, and he continued to do so throughout his career. It is the supervisor's responsibility to train his employees to become supervisors. He must think of himself as a manager and not a "doer," and must concentrate on management tasks. Authority must be delegated along with responsibility; one supervisor cannot effectively manage a large number of employees alone. Specific people should be appointed to handle specific tasks. They in turn report back to the supervisor and as a result, learn which kinds of decisions they can make themselves and which ones should be reserved for the supervisor. This hierarchy of command is necessary and above all, must be instituted openly in order to succeed.

Barbara Halbrook, the third speaker, is Assistant Librarian at Washington University School of Medicine Library in St. Louis. She is in charge of the library's daily operation, which includes supervision of public services, technical services and the office, as well as automation; in all, she heads a staff of forty-seven people. Her experience is similar to Tomczak's in that she was promoted "from within" and had been working at the library for several years. In her opinion, supervising former peers has its advantages: everyone is familiar and the problem of adjusting to a supervisor brought in from outside the library is thus avoided.

The difficulties she experienced in changing from employee to supervisor were ones of personal adjustment. She found it difficult to relinquish her old reference job. As a supervisor, she had to get others to do the work, even though she missed doing it herself. She also realized she was spending too much time in the reference library and neglecting the other departments under her direction.

Halbrook was surprised to find that her social position had changed. People were still friendly, but in a new way. She was not invited to lunch as often as she had been before her promotion, and was excluded from staff "gripe sessions." The staff members were wary of her past relationship with them and attempted to use their former friendship to gain information. She had to be careful to compromise neither old trusts nor new responsibilities; she could not be as casual as before. In attempting to compensate for the new professional distance imposed by other staff, she withdrew from the group. This was not a good solution either, as she was then accused of being bigheaded and secretive.

Halbrook also found that she had to establish an entirely new working relationship with the other administrators in the library: they were no longer "them," but "us." She had to overcome her reluctance to express a personal opinion and at the same time learn when to defer. All of these adjustments took time and she occasionally felt sorry for herself.

The sudden role of authority was also hard to get used to. She had to be objective when recommending salary increases and performing job evaluations of former coworkers; she knew the staff too well. She feels now that, during her adjustment, she perhaps leaned *too* far toward absolute objectivity — but has come to realize that it is impossible to please everyone.

As a result of her new role, Halbrook discovered that, rather than thinking of the library on a personal or departmental basis, she began to view it as a whole. For instance, when the library copier had been placed in the reference department, she and her coworkers had been upset; the perspective afforded by her new position, however, has enabled her to understand and approve of the reasons for such a decision.

As a result of these personal changes, Halbrook feels that she has become less flexible in terms of a job change. She has become accustomed to making decisions and delegating authority, and would not feel comfortable changing back to supervisee. The transition from employee to supervisor seems to her to be a one-way street.

Marian McMahon, Head of the Copy Cataloging Unit of Northwestern University Library, gave her personal history: she trained as a flight instructor and then traveled, and at the age of forty-five — following twenty years as a housewife — decided she wanted a job, and took one as a copy cataloger at Northwestern University. The cataloging unit subsequently split and she was chosen to head part of it; there are three senior and five junior staff members under her supervision. She feels that being older than the people she supervises helps to establish authority.

The problems McMahon encountered were a result of seeking a balance between her former role as "one of the boys" and her new position of authority. She found it difficult to take herself seriously; she felt she was not supervisory material and expected her employees to ignore her when she gave them an order. When giving instructions she found it helpful to clarify that she was not simply making a suggestion and to observe the reactions of the person being instructed. She tried to hearken back to her days as an "underdog" in order to avoid making the same mistakes her past supervisors had.

Her attitude toward her former coworkers changed also. The news that an employee was leaving the library for a new job or to attend library school was no longer greeted with enthusiasm; now all she could think about was the annoyance and problems of interviewing, hiring and training a replacement. McMahon noted the conflict inherent in the supervisor's position, i.e., the sense of duty to encourage staff to progress in their careers and the problems caused by the resulting job vacancies.

McMahon misses cataloging work. She fears becoming a "closet cataloger," sneaking particularly sticky problems off the top of the assignment pile in order to handle them herself. The new job-related tasks are not always pleasant. She finds that employee evaluations are terribly embarrassing situations and the horrendous amount of paperwork makes her feel that she is getting nowhere (although in retrospect, she admits it has value).

McMahon has instituted staff meetings with her employees, which she holds immediately following administrative staff meetings. The higher-echelon meetings are enjoyable because they present her with a broader view of the library, and she can see the progress being made in other departments. She personally handles all training of new employees. In this way, she pointed out, if something is being done wrong, at least the entire staff is doing it wrong the same way — and "that's consistency." Often she finds that she learns something in the training process. In conclusion, McMahon offered the consolation that time cures the fears and the unfamiliarity; endure — if you hang in there long enough, you may be promoted.

The final speaker, Tony Siciliano, is the Head of Circulation at the Skokie Public Library. Unlike the others, Siciliano did not have to adjust to a change in status from employee to supervisor; he was hired into his present position directly from library school. As he was replacing a woman with twenty years of experience, the first problem he encountered was to accustom the staff to having a man as department head.

To learn his new job and to get to know his staff, Siciliano began by holding both conferences with each employee, and staff meetings in which he openly announced his own anxiety about being new and requested the staff's support. He then worked a few weeks in every job in the department in order to gain an understanding of what was being done and to suggest improvements, which were primarily aimed at eliminating drudgery.

He believes that job descriptions and performance evaluations are his most important responsibilities. As no job descriptions had ever been written, his staff wrote them, and also compiled an operations and procedures manual. At the Skokie Library, job evaluations had been used only for determining pay raises, but Siciliano felt that regular evaluation ought to be made standard policy. He now performs job evaluations daily and makes every attempt to reinforce the positive behavior of his employees. He also instituted a formal quarterly evaluation process in which his staff evaluates him and themselves; then he evaluates them and they compare notes. He finds this to be a good approach to reinforcing the goals of the library as a whole, the goals of the department within the library, and goals as structural changes.

RICHARD CALABRESE

Chairman
Communication Arts and Sciences Department
Rosary College
River Forest, Illinois

Interaction Skills and the Modern Supervisor

The responsibilities of modern supervisors have been expanded to include planning, operating and controlling the production and personnel functions of their departments. Supervisors also have a strong voice in decision-making, job design, job analysis, and quality control among their own staff. Personnel responsibilities have been extended to include training, counseling and managing the development of workers. Supervisors perform all these functions within an organizational, economic and social context. Regardless, however, of the supervisor's tasks, organizational skills and awareness of the interrelationships of human, organizational and social factors, unless he is able to *model* and utilize sophisticated communication skills when interacting with his staff, he is likely to be inefficient in maintaining optimum production and service. The purpose of this paper, therefore, is to discuss the application of the general principles of communication to the specific context of employee supervision in libraries.

PRINCIPLES OF COMMUNICATION

Below are three specific principles and suggestions based on behavioral science data for improving supervisory communication. However, it is not enough simply to know and appreciate communication principles; they must be translated into appropriate behavior. Each of us is different, and there are no perfect blueprints for the ideal communication style. Supervisors must decide how to incorporate the principles in a way that is comfortable for them, taking into consideration such variables as the personalities of their subordinates, the particular organizational climate of their library, and individual personality. The reader should be cautioned further that one does not become an "expert" human relations specialist instantly, and that some dissatisfaction in early attempts to change communication behavior should be expected. Old habits are hard to change, but if one is willing to make a conscientious effort to increase communication competence, he will eventually succeed.

Principle 1

Meanings are in people — not in words. Words are merely symbols. No matter what or how something is said, no one derives exactly the same meaning the speaker intended from the words used. There are several implications here for supervisors. For instance, when passing instructions downward to the subordinate, it is unwise for the supervisor simply to ask if the message has been understood. More than likely the recipient will respond positively. It may be that he doesn't want to appear stupid in the boss's eyes, or he may honestly believe he has fully understood the message. In any case, requesting the other to paraphrase important instructions is a far more efficient way to verify that both persons understand each other. One will learn, however, that most people go through life believing they are communicating fully when, in fact, the amount of accurate transmission is closer to 50 or 60 percent.

A second implication involves upward communication, that is, messages sent from subordinates to the supervisor. The behavioral literature refers to this phenomenon as the "good news barrier to communication." Apparently, no one wants to bring "bad" news to the boss; consequently, information passed upward is often slanted positively. Supervisors need to compensate for this by rechecking information, seeking verification from a variety of sources, and creating a climate that permits their subordinates to be candid without fear of rejection, insult or humiliation. Supervisors ultimately are decision-makers, and decision-makers need *accurate* information — both good and bad. A staff that is afraid to reveal its true insights and feelings will hamper the quality of the supervisor's decisions.

Principle 2

Worker satisfaction, and ultimately production and services, are affected considerably by the social climate that exists among the staff, between the staff and supervisor, and between one department's staff and another's. Conflict within a work group is inevitable. The enlightened supervisor will expect it, prepare for it, and use it to obtain greater awareness of the various aspects of the problem at hand. Studies in group dynamics indicate that the greater the variety of perspectives in a group, the greater is that group's potential for *synergy,* that is, group decisions that are qualitatively superior to those of the most resourceful group member working alone. In other words, group conflict and heterogeneity are actually an asset to a supervisor skilled in group dynamics, the techniques of participative decision-making, and the means of achieving group consensus. Jay Hall and Irving L. Janis have written outstanding articles on the subject which include practical suggestions.[1]

Principle 3

When conflict is confronted and dealt with, the supervisor can anticipate an increase in hostility and tension; however, this anxiety is ordinarily short-lived and is followed by long-term harmony. In work groups, social concerns take precedence over task concerns. Individuals are unable to work optimally when experiencing some social concern such as feelings of humiliation, hurt, anger or frustration. Unless the social concern is perceived by the supervisor and dealt with, production and services are likely to suffer. It takes a supervisor with well-developed communication skills to handle this situation. Those who have such abilities are generally the most successful, representing departments with records of high production, superior service and *esprit de corps.* Confronting conflict is best done through the creation of a supportive climate.

Such a climate is one in which individuals feel comfortable expressing themselves openly, and in which opposing views are heard without defensiveness. Nonsupportive climates create defensiveness and are inefficient. Once an individual's defenses are aroused, he is no longer able to listen rationally, but will instead concentrate on his own feelings of anger, revenge, rejection and humiliation.

CREATING A SUPPORTIVE CLIMATE

The discussion which follows describes some behavioral techniques, culled from the communication literature, that have proven to be essential for creating a supportive climate. As many of them as possible should be employed simultaneously whenever the supervisor needs to discuss with a subordinate a topic likely to create tension and anxiety.

1. The supervisor should describe his perceptions of the situation rather than evaluate the person involved. For example, he might say to the evening librarian in the children's room, "Circulation has gone down 25 percent during the evening hours over the last three weeks." While this comment might make the evening librarian tense, it would probably be less threatening than if he had said, "You people are goofing off at night. You are all lazy goldbricks." By describing only objective facts, without making personal evaluations or engaging in name-calling, the other is allowed to respond to the objective facts. When a

person believes the criticism is against him personally, his natural instinct is to become defensive and fight back.

2. The problem-oriented supervisor is more likely to reduce a subordinate's defensiveness than one who is controlling and manipulative. For example, the former might say, "There seems to be a problem during the evening. What can be done to raise circulation?" A manipulative supervisor, for example, might begin with a series of questions for which he already had the answers, merely trying to get the staff to acknowledge his perspective: "Isn't it true that last month's circulation was 25 percent higher? Isn't it true that patrons have complained about the rudeness of the staff?" The primary responsibility of the supervisor is to increase production and quality of service, neither of which is ordinarily aided through reprimand or punishment.

3. A supportive climate is fostered when the supervisor is empathic in dealing with a staff member, rather than unfeeling and disinterested in the other's perceptions of the situation. In behavioral terms, *empathy* is more than just "putting oneself in the other's shoes." Rather, it is making an effort to appreciate the other's perspective and then *verbally* sharing his concern. Instead of silently suspecting that a subordinate is anxious and nervous about some problem, the supervisor might ask him if this is so. The act of verbalizing the empathic concern is likely to cause the other to infer interest and warmth on the supervisor's part, which in turn causes him to want to continue communicating. Open channels of communication which encourage subordinates to reveal their concerns to the supervisor are the primary ingredient of a healthy work environment.

   Good listening skills are directly related to empathizing. Before one can make a sincere effort to appreciate the problems of another, he has to listen, not only to the content, but to the underlying feelings. Supervisors who know how to listen have learned that once a subordinate has had an opportunity to clear his own mental agenda, he is much more receptive to the suggestions of a supervisor. He can sit back and listen, for now he knows the "boss" has heard his side and appreciates his position and rationale.

4. The supportive climate is maintained when the subordinate perceives no intent on the part of the supervisor to emphasize relative rank and status. Each person knows who is in the position to reward and punish, but when supervisors underscore their rank, they tend to put subordinates on the defensive.

   In each of these guidelines, the accompanying nonverbal communication is as important as the verbal. Recent studies indicate that approximately 65-75 percent of the meaning abstracted from communication originates from nonverbals.[2] When the verbal and the nonverbal do not support one another, the listener tends to trust his interpretation of the nonverbal. If one is verbally making an effort to paraphrase another and to empathize, but at the same time is looking at his watch or nervously fingering his telephone or car keys, the other will surely decide that the speaker would rather be doing something else.

With regard to the emphasis on relative status, nonverbals are particularly influential. Supervisors who expect employees to stand while they sit, who plan their offices so that their superior rank is evident in trophies or parchment, or who arrange special barriers around themselves to keep others from getting too close are likely to be fostering a defensive climate within their work group.

5. In maintaining a supportive climate, the supervisor must be careful to avoid making judgments prior to hearing all sides of an issue. Perhaps the four most important words a supervisor can use when confronting a subordinate with a problem are: I may be wrong. When the supervisor lets a subordinate know that he recognizes the fact that reality may be structured differently according to one's perspective, and that he is willing to withhold judgment until all views have been considered, that supervisor will be securing a supportive climate. If the subordinate suspects that the supervisor has a preconceived notion of the "true" facts, and that he alone will decide what is "right," the subordinate will probably accommodate by saying "all the right things," but never revealing his true concerns, anxieties or questions.

Rarely will anyone change his mind simply by being asked to, told to or argued with. A person is not likely to see a situation differently as long as he feels threatened and in need of defending himself. Supervisors need to control their own ego-building desire to get the upper hand, to point out weaknesses in another person's point of view. Weaknesses — when they are important — need to be revealed; however, this can be done in a way that leaves the other person's ego intact. Every opportunity must be taken to make the other person feel respected and valued.

REFERENCES

1. Hall, Jay. "Decisions, Decisions, Decisions," *Psychology Today* 5:51-54+, Nov. 1971; and Janis, Irving L. "Groupthink," *Psychology Today* 5:43-46+, Nov. 1971.

    2. Knapp, Mark L. *Nonverbal Communication in Human Interaction.* New York, Holt, Rinehart & Winston, 1972; and Mehrabian, Albert. *Silent Messages.* Belmont, Calif., Wadsworth Publishing, 1971.

ELAINE M. ALBRIGHT
Executive Director
Lincoln Trail Libraries System
Champaign, Illinois

Handling Employee Problems

The most effective means of handling employee problems is to recognize and eliminate their probable cause before they arise. The authors of other papers included in these proceedings have provided guidance for avoiding manager/employee problems on a daily basis. If the conditions they discuss are monitored, there should be little need for "handling employee problems." In order to identify a problem, a supervisor must know and be sensitive to employees' needs as well as have a comprehensive view of organizational goals. The way in which each employee's role fits into the overall plan of service should be well defined. With this information, an insightful manager can identify both real and potential problems and deal with them appropriately.

The following areas must be investigated before a supervisor can begin to manage employees:

1. *Job analysis:* Is the job necessary to the organizational goal? Why? How does it fit into the total plan of service? Is it doable? Have the necessary tools been provided? Is the job adequately organized? Are there well-defined areas of responsibility?
2. *Selection:* Do the applicants have the aptitude and potential to do the job? From what can be determined during the interview, do the applicants' personal goals relate to the stated organizational goals?
3. *Orientation and training:* Has the employee been provided the information necessary to do the job?

4. *Incentives:* Do the rewards of the job meet the needs of the employee — especially the most important need, the need to feel worthwhile?
5. *Appraisal of performance:* Is there an agreement between the manager and the employee to discuss how well the job is being performed?

While this framework for analyzing work situations is always applicable, the answers to the questions asked in each step do change. Therefore, the supervisory approach must be updated daily. If done regularly, supervision will not take much time, and time may actually be saved through the avoidance of problems.

If this formula is effective for avoiding or controlling problems, then why does every manager have problems? No manager ever has complete control over the factors which influence the work environment. Often the cause of a problem is clouded by employee complaints that are not closely related to or associated with the real problem. Some of these areas are:

1. *Social:* It is estimated that by 1980 one out of every four persons entering the labor force will have a college degree. Motivating overqualified people to do routine work is no easy matter. Also, the change in lifestyles experienced over the past twenty-five years influences employees' reactions to their work environment. Most people expect their jobs to be consistent with their lifestyles. Basic value changes influence the traditional "work ethic." The generation gap is widening. One can no longer expect even siblings born within a few years of each other to have the same values.
2. *Economic and technological:* Inflation influences the amount any organization can afford to pay its employees. Advances in technology determine whether or not a routine, boring job can be automated.
3. *Legal:* Equal Employment Opportunity, the Occupational Safety and Health Administration, labor unions, and affirmative action control the amount of flexibility an employer has in hiring and in creating a work environment.
4. *Organization itself:* Large organizations are often forced, for economic and efficiency reasons, to utilize civil service or other standardized personnel practices to insure fairness and equality throughout the organization. Job classification, hiring guidelines, pay plans, work hours, etc., are all outlined for supervisors to follow.

In the real world, for a variety of reasons, problems do arise. It is fair to say that a mark of effective supervision is not that there are never problems, but rather that problems can be handled without disrupting the entire organization. As a supervisor gains a reputation for being fair, open and responsive, the number of problems should diminish, for, as a result, he often will be given the benefit of any doubt in situations that would otherwise lead to resentment or conflict.

The first step in dealing with a problem is to determine why it arose in the first place. This may be the hardest part of the process, since things are almost never what they appear to be on the surface. It is important to examine the work situation objectively. Have all the obstacles to work performance been removed? Obstacles are defined as conditions that prevent job performance: inadequate time, instructions, tools or resources; conflicting orders (too many bosses); or too much red tape.

A distinction should be made between dissatisfiers and obstacles. Dissatisfiers cloud issues but do not prevent the performance of a job (examples are inadequate parking, pay or fringe benefits). They are obstacles to work gratification, but if motivated, an employee will still do the job. A dissatisfier is often a symptom of the problem, not a reason, and it is important to be aware of the difference. A dissatisfier can upset people, but resolution of the condition does not necessarily result in employee motivation. The opposite of dissatisfaction is not satisfaction, but the absence of dissatisfaction.

If obstacles to job performance are discovered, they should be removed — if possible. Some may be beyond the control of the supervisor (for example, bottlenecks in other departments or unpredictable workflow), but it is still important to recognize such problems and attempt to solve them. If a situation cannot be changed, admitting that it is beyond one's control and making the best of it will still be helpful. To continue to pursue a lost cause will frustrate both the supervisor and the employees and result in a loss of confidence in the supervisor's ability to handle problems. Achievement-motivated people will continue to work as best they can. Performance should be evaluated with consideration for the working conditions.

It may be that a job is doable and necessary, but extremely routine. Someone doing such a job may have more time than anyone needs to think up problems. It is wise to consider automating such a position as soon as possible.

Employee problems related to working conditions are the easiest to solve. Removal of an obstacle, once identified, generally eliminates the problem. Once an effective work structure is set up, problems can be anticipated by monitoring changes in external factors affecting the job. The greatest challenge of supervision is in dealing with employee motivational problems unrelated to the working conditions. Resolution of these problems will vary according to the personalities involved. Every employee comes to a job with certain needs and expectations. These are often not determined by the job or organization, but rather by past and present life experiences. Family, peers, and religious and educational experiences are most influential in determining a person's work attitudes. These attitudes will not be changed easily, but if recognized and understood, they can be used by an experienced and responsive supervisor to organizational advantage.

I believe — and this belief has been reinforced by experience — that all people need recognition and must be made to feel worthwhile. We all are motivated to perform in a way we hope will fulfill this need. What makes individuals feel worthwhile varies. Also, *who* recognizes them makes a difference in their response. Handling "people problems" requires skills other than those taught in library schools, but our success as librarians and information specialists depends on our ability to provide services through the combined efforts of the entire library staff. Getting people to do what is expected with minimum supervision is a key to successful library administration.

Most people perform in a way *they* perceive as good for the organization. They do this in order to be treated as worthwhile by their supervisors and the organization. An effective supervisor finds out what will make each employee feel needed and attempts to supply it. If a supervisor does not voluntarily do so, employees will force recognition by performing in such a way that their supervisor must acknowledge them. An employee's need to be recognized will be manifested in one of two ways: (1) *detractive* — negative performance that will require the supervisor to acknowledge the behavior, and (2) *contributive* — a positive approach furthering organizational goals. A strictly problem-oriented administration may, through its recognition only of problems, generate more problems from employees seeking recognition.

An effective supervisor must convince his employees that his goals and objectives are also theirs. How this is done depends on the supervisor's opinion of human nature — of why people react the way they do. A supervisor's personal attitudes are central to success in handling motivational problems. In order to relate to the problems of employees, a supervisor must understand himself, his attitudes and why he reacts to or interprets behavior the way he does. Just as employees come to a job with needs and expectations, so also does a supervisor manage his department according to a set of standards, expectations and attitudes acquired from his family, peers, education and religion. A manager needs the confidence of his employees in his ability to deal with them in a fair, open and reassuring manner. However, he will not inspire trust if he does not trust himself. If a person is uncomfortable with himself, flexibility and openness, the two most important characteristics of a good manager, will be difficult if not impossible to achieve. Defensiveness is often the mark of the person unsure of his own identity. Defensive managers are often the *cause* of problems, since they tend to overreact and lose perspective when faced with change, minor problems or conflict. If, in the course of self-evaluation, a person discovers he does not really like people, it would be best for him to avoid supervisory responsibilities altogether.

Knowing oneself is not a guarantee against employee problems, but it is essential for anticipating and recognizing the source of problems when dealing with people of certain temperaments. It is advantageous for a supervisor to hire the kind of persons with whom he can work comfortably. No one can relate to everyone; however, while supervisors cannot expect to "like" or be "friends" with all their employees, they must be able to respect the humanity of others. People have a right to expect no less, and will surely sense negative attitudes. An inability to relate to people will prevent a supervisor from satisfying his employees' need to feel worthwhile. I am not encouraging or condoning discriminatory hiring practices, but supervisors must be realistic about their attitudes and not ask for trouble by ignoring "gut" feelings about a person during the interview.

What happens when problems with an employee continue after obstacles to job performance have been removed, his ability to do the job has been determined, and motivational techniques have been tried? Admit the failure to relate to the needs of this employee and deal with the problem in the best way possible. I recommend to managers the following initial steps: Be absolutely sure that the situation has been viewed as clearly, fairly and objectively as possible. Run through the last five steps outlined at the beginning of this paper. Review the situation with a respected supervisor who is not directly involved. Outline the problem and the solutions that have been attempted. Listen to and analyze the advice or response given. Implement any useful suggestions. If none of these are successful, a manager should talk to his superior. Outline the problem, the solutions attempted and the intended next step. The superior should understand and support the proposed resolution. If the problem cannot be resolved, it may well fall into his hands, and it is never advisable to be overruled in the handling of a problem. Once input has been sought and a manager is convinced that he is being fair, he should talk to the employee.

Boyd outlines what should be avoided in an employee/supervisor discussion of problems. For each approach to be avoided, he supplies an alternative.

What to avoid	*What to do*
Sarcasm	Consider feelings of employees.
Loss of temper	Cool down, analyze each situation.
Humiliating an employee	Show confidence in the employee's ability to make necessary changes.
Profanity	Carefully explain the nature of the violation and the correction expected.
Public reprimands	*Always* reprimand in private.
Threats and bluffs	Outline specific consequences of future violations, and follow through.
Showing favoritism	Give every employee fair treatment.
Delay tactics	Give prompt attention to violations.
Unduly harsh penalties	Define the objective of disciplinary action.
Inconsistent enforcement	Deal promptly with all violations of rules.[1]

It is always important for managers to listen to the employee's reaction to the manager's observation of the problem. It may be that the employee perceives the problem differently and discussion may lead to a common resolution. For this approach to work, a supervisor must be flexible and prepared to compromise. Asking an employee for his opinion with no intention of accepting it is worse than not asking at all. Occasionally an employee will offer an explanation worthy of thought or investigation. Managers shouldn't hesitate to admit that the view is new. The employee should be told that his views will be considered and that he will have a response by a certain time. The situation should then be re-examined in light of the additional information. The next time manager and employee talk — and this *must* be soon — they will both be sure they are talking about the same thing. I have used this approach with employees several times and although I have seldom changed my original thinking, the employees have been convinced that I seriously reconsidered the situation. For this reason they are more willing to accept my approach to the resolution of the problem.

It is important that, in the course of the problem-oriented interview, the employee acknowledge that he understands the manager's statements and the improvements expected. This does not necessarily mean agreement or acceptance, since this rarely happens, but such a discussion accomplishes several things for both the employee and the supervisor. It clarifies the job and the supervisor's expectations of performance; it gives the employee an opportunity to communicate his needs and problems to the supervisor; and most importantly, both learn where they stand in relation to each other. The supervisor, by emphasizing the need for performance, acknowledges that the person and his position are important and worthwhile to the organization.

At the end of the discussion, the employee should feel that the problem lies with his actions, not with him personally. The manager must continue to treat that employee just as he does everyone else. The human temptation to avoid this employee until he meets the manager's standards must be avoided. It may be difficult, but the supervisor *must* act as if the problem employee is a worthwhile member of the staff. A disciplinary discussion should never be held on Friday as this will leave no time for reassurance. There will be too much time over the weekend for defensive attitudes to develop.

Managers should be prepared to follow through with appropriate disciplinary action if the established criteria are not met. Disciplinary action taken as a result of the discussion should *never* be a surprise. It should be clear that if X continues, Y will surely happen. My attitudes when handling employee problems are:

1. The first time: The employee didn't know better. I must have failed to communicate my expectations. I clarify the situation immediately.
2. The second time: The employee was careless. I notify the employee of problems both verbally and in writing.
3. The third time: The employee will be looking for another job.

Although most of the literature on discipline emphasizes the need to administer positive discipline, the most common interpretation of discipline is punishment, and that is almost never positive. Disciplining an employee always provokes negative reactions. Discipline is a last effort to change the actions of an employee who has not responded to positive incentives. When I take disciplinary action or issue a reprimand, I am admitting my failure to relate to the positive needs of that employee.

There *are* positive outcomes of properly administered discipline. The way a supervisor handles discipline will help to set the tone of the office. Avoiding disciplining employees that require it frustrates those who do not need discipline to perform. Frustration leads to demotivation and a leveling of performance. The value of discipline, then, lies more in reinforcing the rules and regulations being followed by those motivated than in making a point with the disciplined employee. We all are concerned about getting fair treatment. It is not good for morale to see someone consistently getting away with breaking rules we are told we must follow. At the same time, we are not comfortable seeing unduly harsh treatment for minor offenses. Discipline should fit the offense. In deciding whether or not discipline is appropriate, take into consideration the seriousness of the offense, the action itself, and the past performance of the offender. Is this person normally a motivated worker? What was the intent of his action? What discipline has been administered in similar cases?

Discipline should also be timely. A manager must not watch a recurring problem for weeks before calling attention to it. Each time it is ignored the manager, by his silence, is condoning the action. Delayed discipline may also seem arbitrary and personal. The timing, tone and manner used in administering discipline are all-important. A time should be chosen when the manager's temper is controlled and he is alone with the employee. If the manager is too angry with the employee when the offense occurs, the employee should be told that he will be seen later, and this meeting should take place as soon as possible.

The manager's approach should cause as little damage to his relationship with the employee as possible. He should speak specifically, emphasizing the problems with the employee's action and why it is unacceptable. Once the action is corrected, the manager/employee relationship should be righted. A person reacts differently to being told he has fallen down on the job than he does to being told he is useless and a loafer. All employees resent downgrading aimed at them personally and will not forget it.

According to Dowling and Sayles, discipline accomplishes a strengthening of a rule through enforcement, a correcting of the individual's breach of the rule, and a warning that the individual must comply or face more serious consequences. This acts as a reminder to all employees of a rule's existence and the gravity with which it is regarded, as well as a reassurance for the vast majority who respect the rule out of positive motivation to perform well.[2]

It is the result, not the discipline itself, that is positive. Douglas McGregor advanced the "hot stove rule" for effective discipline: it should be similar to the reaction one gets from touching a hot stove — immediate, impersonal and consistent. If a supervisor does a good job of disciplining, the employee may feel resentful, but he'll also feel somewhat guilty and foolish about his resentment — as though he had kicked the stove for burning him.[3]

While discipline can produce positive results, the repeated need to discipline an employee for willful, substandard performance will have an adverse effect on office morale. Very soon the manager's actions will not be taken seriously. Each time an employee slips below standards, the standards themselves begin to slip. Time spent dealing with a problem employee is time taken from other administrative duties. The ability to motivate employees depends on the manager's credibility in handling situations that work counter to organizational goals. If control over the library staff is to be maintained, either the problem or the problem employee must be eliminated. Department heads often hesitate or resist firing unsatisfactory employees because they feel it is too difficult. The tension and resentment which results in them and the rest of the staff will drain vital job enthusiasm. The entire workflow will slow with the drop in morale. Managers must not be foolish enough to think that they can ignore a problem situation or that functions around the problem will continue normally — they will not.

Reasonable standards of acceptable performance must be set and employees who willfully fall below them must be eliminated. Of course, severe handling of willful noncompliance must not preclude humane consideration for contributing factors. Lack of humanity on the part of a supervisor will be noted as surely as lack of consistency and it will color employee relations.

There are restraints and guidelines in structured systems, such as civil service and union contracts, which are designed to assure fair treatment for everyone. These systems acknowledge that the supervisor is responsible for enforcing rules, assigning work, running the department, and representing management and the organization's goals. However, some formal employee grievance procedure is usually provided. Unions strive to eliminate inequities and provide employees with benefits they could not achieve individually; they also work to equalize the division of power between management and employee. Supervisory flexibility may be impaired by formal contractual limitations. In some unionized situations, supervisors have lost much of their power to administer discipline; this has been reserved for the labor relations board. The techniques discussed in this paper should remain useful in a union or civil service situation, but they must be adapted to the more formal procedures. It is essential to know a contract in detail in order to act within its rules. All actions should be documented. A person's position as a responsive but effective supervisor can be maintained even though his actions may be restricted or delayed.

REFERENCES

1. Boyd, Bradford B. *Management-Minded Supervision.* 2d ed. New York, McGraw-Hill, 1976, p. 203.
2. Dowling, William F., and Sayles, Leonard R. *How Managers Motivate: The Imperatives of Supervision.* 2d ed. New York, McGraw-Hill, 1978, p. 160.
3. *See* ibid., p. 161.

AGNES M. GRIFFEN

Deputy Library Director
Tucson Public Library
Tucson, Arizona

Equal Employment Opportunity Principles and Affirmative Action Practices in Library Supervision

The purpose of this paper is to share information I have gathered through experience and reading which I hope will illustrate why affirmative action can be sound management. This information should enable the reader to:

1. gain some understanding of the legal and social bases of equal employment opportunity and the need for taking affirmative action in the management of libraries;
2. know where to find basic information on equal employment opportunity and affirmative action;
3. apply equal opportunity principles in all areas of supervisory practice; and
4. provide leadership in developing support for, writing and implementing an affirmative action plan for the library in which you work.

First, I will briefly review definitions and legal bases, and will try to show why equal employment opportunity in libraries is necessary to provide equal access to information. Three reasons why libraries need to take affirmative action will be followed by a discussion of the impact of equal opportunity principles and affirmative action practices in these areas: interviewing, selecting, training, developing, evaluating, promoting, rewarding, disciplining and terminating employees. Then I will emphasize the value and importance of having the protection and guidance of a written affirmative action plan. I will outline some basic, but not necessarily easy, steps to take in ensuring that your library will operate by such a plan, and suggest some ideas for "action programs" libraries can employ to resolve problems identified through various surveys and studies.

In conclusion, I will share some personal reflections, hopes and objectives for achieving both quality and equity in library personnel administration. My hypothesis, then, is that affirmative action is good management. The final proof of this hypothesis is the responsibility of each of us as we practice the art of good supervision.

DEFINITIONS AND SOURCES OF INFORMATION

Equal employment opportunity is the law. More accurately, it is a condition that someday may exist in organizations that have succeeded in eliminating not only blatant discrimination, but also covert practices which at present unfairly limit certain individuals' opportunities to be hired or effectively utilized in the organization. The goal of equal opportunity laws is to create an "employment environment whereby all employees and employment applications are judged on individual merit without regard to race, color, national origin, religion, sex, age, physical or mental disability, or political affiliation."[1] Employers should disregard all other characteristics that are not job-related, such as sexual or affectional preference. Although the legal mandate for this does not yet exist at the federal level, it has been legitimized by some state and local legislation and is included in American Library Association (ALA) policy.

The achievement of equal opportunity in libraries of all types is hindered by a notable lack of awareness that a problem in this area even exists. If the issue is addressed at all by library administrators, it is often perceived only as a federal regulatory nuisance that threatens the receipt of federal funds and is designed to make it difficult or impossible for managers to manage. This abysmal situation is perpetuated by library managers who fail to assess accurately or objectively their own level of performance in personnel administration. "After all, no one in this organization, and certainly not myself, would ever discriminate against anyone," is the usual defensive response of those finally charged with violation of the fair employment law.

Unfortunately, it is often at this point, rather than much earlier, when endless bureaucratic interrogatories, lost administrative time, and court costs could still be avoided, that library managers or boards admit they must comply with the law and eliminate discriminatory practices. A court order does not, of course, serve to motivate administrators strongly enough to result in any meaningful change beyond a written plan. What a pity to have quotas imposed and management flexibility severely limited when all this could be avoided through sound management and planning, direct confrontation and problem-solving sessions with employees, and an effective affirmative action program!

If equal opportunity is seen as the goal, then affirmative action is the means, to be implemented through programs to improve the lot of those discriminated against in the past. The problem that exists in libraries, as well as in other organizations, is that we have not yet learned how to "translate the various regulations into positive personnel practices and procedures."[2] This is compounded by general ignorance of basic personnel management principles among some top library administrators. The well-managed libraries in this country now employ professional personnel administrators, a trend which I applaud. While many library directors' only response to the challenge of compliance is to complain about the lack of qualified minority applicants for professional positions, through affirmative action programs a few leaders in the profession are attempting to remedy past discrimination and prevent future discrimination. Most importantly, those who give it some thought are beginning to see that "an affirmative action program can be used as a management tool to help clarify institutional personnel policies. In addition to showing commitment to upholding the laws, it provides a way to set up procedures so that discrimination practices do not take place and the rights of [all] individuals are protected."[3]

Federal and state laws and regulations as well as local ordinances provide the legal basis for affirmative action. The most important federal law protecting minorities, women and other groups is the Equal Opportunity Act of 1972, which extends the coverage of Title VII of the Civil Rights Act of 1964 to state and local governments with more than fifteen employees. Universities also are prohibited from discrimination on the basis of sex by Title IX of the Higher Education Act of 1972, which extends the provisions of the Equal Pay Act of 1963 to executive, administrative and professional employees of academic institutions. Handicapped persons and Vietnam-era and disabled veterans are protected by the 1973 Rehabilitation Act amendments of 1974, especially Sections 503 and 504, and the Vietnam Era Veterans Readjustment Act. Other federal statutes supporting equal employment opportunity include the 1967 and 1975 Age Discrimination in Employment Acts and more recent amendments, the 1972 Revenue Sharing Act, the Comprehensive Employment and Training Act of 1973, and various Executive Orders. A detailed summary of major fair employment laws may be found in the 1978 *ALA Yearbook,*[4] and in the 2-volume guidebook for employers, *Affirmative Action and Equal Employment,*[5] available free from the U.S. Equal Employment Opportunity Commission in Washington, D.C.

There is usually much duplication between state and federal laws but more variance may be noted in county or city ordinances. Libraries writing affirmative action plans often cite a local statute establishing an affirmative action plan for the municipality of which they are a unit. Conversely, many libraries have failed to develop their own plans precisely because they feel they are covered under the "umbrella plan," which, of course, is technically true. However, the Equal Employment Opportunity (EEO) Subcommittee of the ALA, established to implement the Equal Employment Opportunity Policy adopted by the ALA Council in 1974, encourages libraries that are part of a larger governmental unit to write departmental plans and implement equal employment opportunity by tailor-making "action programs to rectify any problems applicable to library affirmative action."[6]

Voluntary compliance with equal employment law through the development of a written affirmative action plan is urged in the ALA/EEO Policy, which directs all libraries with fifteen or more employees to submit their plans to the Office for Library Personnel Resources (OLPR), with the reward of being listed in *American Libraries* as having submitted a plan. In accordance with this policy, the EEO Subcommittee has developed "Guidelines for Library Affirmative Action Plans" and on a confidential basis will review plans submitted to OLPR. Detailed critiques by two members of the subcommittee are consolidated into one report that is returned to the library with suggestions for improvements. These guidelines were published in the July/August 1976 issue of *American Libraries,* along with commentaries on the ALA/EEO Policy statement. To date, fewer than thirty libraries have made use of this free service.

Margaret Myers and Elizabeth Dickinson have written the best state-of-the-art summary to date, entitled "Affirmative Action and American Librarianship."[7] An annual review of affirmative action-related developments in libraries is included in the *ALA Yearbook* under the heading "Personnel and Employment: Affirmative Action." In a thoughtful discussion entitled "Equity and Patterns of Library Governance," Michelle Rudy explored efforts to decrease discrimination that have had some influence on management style in libraries.[8] Additional materials for those interested in developing affirmative action plans are available for $1 from OLPR. ALA staff will also answer specific questions pertaining to personnel, give advice on affirmative action, or at least refer you to a knowledgeable source.

WHY LIBRARIES NEED TO TAKE AFFIRMATIVE ACTION

Beyond the obvious reason that affirmative action is required by libraries that accept any federal funds, there are two specific reasons why libraries need to comply with the law in administering library personnel systems. Before discussing these reasons, I want to state that at its best affirmative action is a management attitude based on the belief that every person has the right to and, given the opportunity, is able to achieve his or her innate potential. Affirmative action may be perceived as the bureaucratic translation or expression of the human potentials movement. As Abraham Maslow noted, managers should "assume in all your people the impulse to achieve."[9] I sense that the lack of this attitude toward all applicants and employees is one major factor contributing to the "chilling effect" of discrimination against minorities, the handicapped and women.

I have often wondered at the apparent disinterest in Fourteenth Amendment issues[10] on the part of some library administrators and trustees who take pride in their unbending adherence to First Amendment rights as interpreted for library users in the Library Bill of Rights. Is not equal access to information — free and uncensored — a basic principle of library policy? Why, then, are librarians not concerned as well with equal opportunity in employment, without which equal access for some users may not exist? On a practical level, basic library service cannot be provided to the 12 million or more Spanish-speaking people in this country without affirmative action in recruiting and hiring bilingual librarians. How can deaf patrons truly be served without hiring deaf librarians or, at the very least, learning sign language ourselves? The second and most obvious reason, then, for affirmative action of all kinds in libraries is that, in order to meet the library and information needs of all segments of the public, the library should employ people who can reflect, relate to and communicate with the people in the community it serves.

Involvement of staff at all levels is the basic prerequisite for successful implementation of an affirmative action plan. It is my impression that those few libraries now in compliance with equal employment law generally are those that practice some form of participatory management. However, Rudy warned that:

> Inequity can occur even with participation. . . . It seems unlikely that participation as an alternate form of library governance can ensure equity for minority and women librarians. . . . Nevertheless, participation and equal employment opportunity legislation, like the proverbial carrot and stick (the law to grab attention and the rewards of participation — increases in job satisfaction, morale, feelings of achievement and self-actualization — to keep it), have the potential for creating an environment where equity can flourish.[11]

The underlying problem in implementing an affirmative action plan is that in order to remedy past discrimination based on criteria that are not job-related, such as race or sex, one must set hiring and promotional goals based on those very criteria. This positive action brings those previously discriminated against into the applicant pool as "protected classes," which, in turn, stimulates a negative response on the part of those who previously had been favored, and Bakkes come out of the woodwork. Reverse discrimination may also be seen as a rejection of the ancient Judaeo-Christian ethic that the "sins of the fathers should be visited upon their children." What people fail to realize is that equal opportunity ultimately applies to everyone. In my opinion, and in spite of many confusing and contradictory interpretations, the Bakke decision only confirms this insight. Myers and Lynch concluded that, "The pressures on library administrators to take specific steps in improving employment conditions for women and minorities can also benefit the entire staff by actually forcing the adoption of good management policies, the establishment of concrete goals, and the determination and dissemination of non-discriminatory personnel policies."[12] In simple and positive terms, then, if we do achieve equal employment opportunity in our organizations, in the future we will more often select the right person for the job based only on job-related criteria, and we will be more consistent, objective and fair in our treatment of all employees. This is the third reason for affirmative action.

THE IMPACT OF AFFIRMATIVE ACTION
ON SUPERVISORY RESPONSIBILITIES

No matter how well-meaning people may be, affirmative action in libraries does not just happen, nor can isolated acts of goodwill on the part of individual employees constitute an environment in which equal opportunity can flourish. Affirmative action begins at the top with an officially adopted policy and firm commitment to equal opportunity principles in all management practices, by the library board, director and other top administrators. It is implemented and monitored at all levels of the organization through the chain of command. All members of the organization have a responsibility and should be monitored on their performance in equal employment opportunity areas. Supervisors are held responsible "up the line" for nondiscriminatory practices and equal treatment of all those who report to them. Disciplinary action should be taken for any act of racism, sexism or other violation of fair employment law. Of course, employees themselves, including those in the protected classes, have a responsibility to keep informed and take advantage of educational, training and career opportunities. They need to be sensitive to the frustrations and resentments of others, as well as be willing to share with management ideas for improving organizational effectiveness.[13] Those who do take the initiative and learn and contribute on the job should be suitably rewarded through merit increases and promotion.

It is at the first-line supervisory level that most violations of equal opportunity law occur. Supervisors who realize their responsibilities for implementing affirmative action policies and procedures, many of which perhaps contradict previously held attitudes and beliefs, may act in both deliberate and covert ways that can make the organization vulnerable to charges of discrimination and in some cases to court action. According to Clark and Perlman, a fear exists in these supervisors that the protected classes will receive undue advantages:

> Among the more common manifestations of this fear are: freezing or withholding information that the employee needs to do the job successfully; unfairly evaluating the employee's performance or even establishing unfair standards of performance for the employee; deliberately sabotaging the employee's efforts; and withholding of opportunities for the employee to compete against other, less threatening employees.[14]

It is in these areas of supervisory responsibility that affirmative action poses some problems, but it also carries the potential for significant improvement in the quality of the work environment.

Hiring

In a recent examination of libraries' employee selection processes, David C. Genaway discovered that 71 percent of academic libraries and 41 percent of public libraries reported that affirmative action was " 'somewhat' to 'considerable' a factor at any stage [although] an ethnic minority was hired in exactly the same [5] percent of cases by both groups."[15] If a library has set hiring goals for new employees who meet certain criteria, such as ethnic or racial representation or bilingual abilities, it is often the direct supervisor who is responsible at least in part for the selection decision. This may place the supervisor in a difficult situation, feeling torn between the conviction that only the "most qualified" person should be selected, and the organizational need to build a more representative staff. While ideally there should be no conflict between these two objectives (new minority librarians may be the best-qualified in every respect), in reality the supervisor may feel both compromised and threatened by this dilemma, especially if he or she has had previous experience with a complaint about treatment of a minority or female employee or applicant.

Three basic guidelines for conducting the hiring interview can be of help to the supervisor who wants to do the right thing and stay out of trouble. The first task is to develop a list of questions designed to elicit information on specific qualities, knowledge, skills and abilities basic to performance of the particular job, and then to ask these same job-related questions of all applicants. (For an excellent discussion of what *not* to ask, read Barry Simon's article on "Personnel Selection Practices: Applications and Interviews."[16])

While some different follow-up questions may be asked of certain applicants in order to clarify an incomplete answer, a fairly equal period of time should be allowed for each interview. The third rule is not always possible to follow, but effort should be made to ensure that the hiring panel is representative of the applicants, i.e., interviewers should include minorities, the disabled, males, females, etc. Even if all the applicants are white females, this is a good idea in order to screen out obvious bigots and obtain a broad spectrum of input in the selection process. While an interview by only one person has been upheld in court as not in violation of equal opportunity law,[17] it seems both unwise and shortsighted for libraries to continue such a practice. Not only does it place the organization in jeopardy, but also limits the chances of actually selecting the best, most qualified person for the job. I truly believe this is one case in which the group process is superior.

Training and Development

In the current situation of strict budget limits, hiring freezes, and little or no turnover, some libraries may be unable to hire members of the protected classes, even if they are in the applicant pool. In such a case, the "best chances for compliance [may] lie with more effective utilization of women and minorities currently employed."[18] A utilization analysis chart shows what percentage of each protected class is working at each level of the organization. Most libraries presently do not utilize significant numbers of minorities as librarians, or women as administrators. A typical affirmative action goal for these organizations would be to increase the utilization of women and minorities in these positions through action programs such as better on-the-job training and orientation, career planning, special recruitment efforts, tuition reimbursement for job- or degree-related academic courses, management development programs, and so on. While first-line supervisors may not be responsible for establishing such programs, their support is absolutely essential for successful implementation of an upward mobility program. The supervisor's major role in affirmative action is to assist, encourage and support each employee's efforts to improve or advance on the job. Specifically, schedules can be kept as flexible as possible to accommodate inservice or outside classes, individuals can be counseled about the value of setting career goals, and performance objectives can be designed to develop specific skills needed for promotion. Most importantly, the supervisor may be able to identify specific barriers preventing the employee from achieving greater potential, and to assist both management and employee in overcoming these obstacles.

Performance Evaluation

Performance evaluation has been called "a pivotal element in complaint prevention."[19] It does not occur in a vacuum. Griffen's First Rule of Supervision is: Every supervisor should spend a minimum of fifteen minutes a week listening to and helping in problem-solving with every employee he or she supervises. It is amazing how rarely this happens. It is easy to get so caught up in our own tasks that we ignore those we are supposed to direct and support. The corollary to the above rule could read: Those who cannot find the time to do this should not be supervisors. Performance evaluation without regular communication is a farce. The employee will feel that the supervisor is not familiar enough with the work being done to make a fair judgment. The problem with any performance evaluation system, no matter how carefully designed, is that no one enjoys giving negative feedback, so supervisors put off discussions until they become confrontations. Criticism that falls from the sky like a thunderbolt once every six months, long after the particular incidents needing correction have been forgotten, will not be taken well, can be successfully rebutted, and will not result in improved performance.

Providing immediate feedback is almost as important as learning to listen to the employee. Listening becomes even more important when differences in cultural or ethnic values exist. Multi-cultural communication must be taken seriously since failure to cross these bridges will only feed the paranoia and fear that already may exist on both sides. Sometimes supervisors are afraid to evaluate a minority or handicapped employee for fear of a complaint to the Affirmative Action Office. This is a very real problem, and the only answer is the use of objective and uniform performance standards for evaluating all employees. The lack of such standards is one of the major obstacles to implementing affirmative action in libraries.

Specifying job-related factors is as much the rule in performance evaluation as it is in the hiring process. Standard position descriptions which spell out the functions and responsibilities of each job may be used to develop specific, objective criteria and performance objectives by which both the supervisor and the employee can measure whether and how well the work is being done. Examples are: "Reinforce a minimum of 100 books in an 8-hour day," or "Improve skills in puppetry by using puppets with children during a class visit, story time or program at least once a month." Setting performance objectives with employees can be helpful in motivating them to develop needed skills and overcome obstacles to promotion. During the probationary period, learning basic skills and job duties can be the focus for performance objectives. After basics have been mastered, developmental objectives may be more helpful, and can be tied to participation in training programs or outside courses in a local community college or university, especially if scholarship support is available.

Personnel Actions That Affect Employees' Salaries and Status

Among the more onerous tasks that come with supervisory responsibility are recommendations to the "hiring authority" on giving or withholding merit increases, promoting, demoting, disciplining and terminating (the euphemism for firing). Supervisors should be reminded that they usually do not have the authority to fire anyone, and that consultation with top management, and the personnel office in particular, is advisable for those who want management support for their actions. Supervisors who blackmail employees into obedience by threatening instant termination should themselves be corrected in writing after proper oral warnings have been documented.

The basic rule for successfully carrying out any adverse personnel actions is: documentation, careful communication, special written evaluations, and impartial discipline on a progressively more severe basis for failure to perform. Most important is an attitude on the part of the supervisor of goodwill and a desire to ensure a climate and opportunities for improvement through direct and honest feedback, guidance and correction, no matter how difficult the confrontation may be.

Documentation is important but can be carried too far. If the supervisor constantly takes detailed notes on various behaviors and failures of those being supervised, employees will soon learn to take their own notes to use as protection in filing grievances or written comments on what are perceived as unfair evaluations or other actions on the part of the supervisor. Unfortunately, the supervisor must document an employee's failure to perform because eventually a management decision to take a particular personnel action may be challenged, either through normal grievance channels or through an affirmative action office. The important thing to remember about this particularly painful fact of organizational life is that it applies to everyone. A more positive approach is to document and reward outstanding performance as well as failure. "Assume that everyone prefers to feel important, needed, useful, successful, proud, respected, rather than unimportant, interchangeable, anonymous, wasted, unused, expendable, disrespected."[20] However, this philosophy, combined with wishful thinking, should not be used as an excuse for lack of complete candor and honesty in performance evaluation.

Careful communication in supervision of employees under discipline occurs over a sustained period of time, first at the oral level, documented with a written memorandum describing the specific infraction and warning given. On the occasion of repeated infraction, a written warning should be given — in the presence of a witness — which describes the behavior for which the reprimand is given, details earlier memoranda and actions, notes specific improvements expected within specified time limits, includes an offer of help by the supervisor, and indicates the next, more serious step to be taken if improvement does not occur. Special evaluations, on either the standard performance evaluation form used in the organization or a written memorandum or letter to the employee, may be given at any time, but regular follow-up should occur, meticulously and on time, and improvement should be noted as well. Again, the use of performance objectives is recommended, and some method of daily, weekly or monthly reporting on the employee's progress should be instituted. A journal listing specific actions being taken to achieve improvement objectives could be kept by the employee under discipline. Feedback from coworkers or subordinates may also be incorporated as documentation, but the evaluator should be aware that this may generate reprisal or future hard feelings.

If — after your best efforts to support, encourage and reward improved behavior — you must finally recommend termination or other severe action, you must be able to document all charges and may have to submit to detailed interrogatories from one or more investigatory bodies. This will be an especially difficult problem in organizations that have never fired anyone, as one defense to disciplinary or termination action is to show that the complainant was not treated differently from other employees. This is a general rule to keep in mind when implementing any personnel system or affirmative action plan: treat all employees alike. If an alcoholic black man is finally terminated for abuse of sick leave and drinking on the job, you had better treat your white female alcoholic the same way. This is one area where all of us, without exception, need to check our own biases. We are especially vulnerable in the area of discrimination against the disabled.[21] The fact that we do have prejudices is one more reason for conscious commitment to affirmative action practices in management, with built-in safety mechanisms for feedback and correction. We need to remember that no one is perfect, no matter how "liberal," and we must not react defensively to discrimination charges, for they may stem from our own lack of awareness.

Grievance Procedures and Channels

What happens if, in response to a management action such as discipline, counseling or transfer, the employee suddenly resigns, and just after you have breathed a sigh of relief at this easy solution, you receive a subpoena from the State Attorney General's Office of Civil Rights on a racial, sex, age or reverse discrimination charge? This is known as "constructive discharge" — resignation by the employee because of management harassment or other intolerable or discriminatory conditions of employment. Even if you tried to talk the employee out of resigning, a charge can be filed. You need to keep in mind the possibility that you may have been in error, that your perception of what you were trying to do was different from that of the grieving employee, or that your strategy in dealing with this particular person was wrong. It is also possible that you may have acted correctly. The point is, once a charge is filed, the burden of proof is on the employer.

Grievance procedures can be a useful tool for management audit of affirmative action supervisory practices. The purpose of grievance procedures is problem-solving. Affirmative action grievances usually utilize channels separate from the ordinary run-of-the-mill complaints about working conditions, lack of due process, etc. Supervisors should remember that they are also entitled to use grievance channels. There are occasional employees who may appear to use a charge of discrimination as a way to harass a supervisor. There are also supervisors who are equally mean and nasty to all those they supervise, regardless of race, sex or creed. Investigatory methods should be developed to keep all contingencies in mind. In the future, personnel officers may need some paralegal training. At present, charges of equal opportunity violations must be taken seriously, investigated and reported on, with recommendations made to management for action, either to support the charges and initiate disciplinary and remedial action, or to suggest that the charge is groundless. In the latter case, one must always suggest other channels of recourse to the charging party.

The first recourse is usually to a municipal affirmative action office, which may be able to conduct an outside and perhaps more objective evaluation of the case. If possible, you might try to get them to do the initial investigation for you, especially if you are white and the grievance is filed by a minority, or vice versa. Keep in mind that EEO officers may also have biases.

The next step in filing a discrimination complaint may be with the County Commission on Human Relations or the State Attorney General's Office of Civil Rights. When a complainant files at three or four levels simultaneously, a situation both possible and common, the federal EEO Commission Regional Office will usually defer the investigation to the next level down, from federal to state, or the Attorney General or local commission may defer it to the municipal office. Findings at a lower level are often upheld at a higher level without additional investigation. Employers charged can expect to receive in the mail either a subpoena to appear in person and testify at the Attorney General's office, or a long list of questions or "interrogatories" to which detailed and documented responses must be written, or both. If the investigator concludes that the employer is probably guilty of the charge, a "right to sue" letter may be given to the charging party. If the EEO Commission investigation supports the charge, the commission itself may choose to support legal action, especially if a precedent-setting case is needed, but often the complainant must pay the costs. If the employer is found guilty, however, he or she must pay legal costs as well as back pay or other compensation to make the complainant "whole." A decision either to submit to conciliation or fight the charges must be made pragmatically by top management, the library board if it is administrative in function, or the city manager, dean or other administrator in the parent organization. An agreement to conciliate or settle out of court may not be seen by management as an admission of guilt but as the most cost-effective way to resolve the problem.

One warning is in order. While employees may have access to established, well-publicized channels for grievance, they also have the right to ignore internal mechanisms and to file first with an outside, higher-level agency. It is also wise to remember that they have the right as citizens to complain to elected officials and probably should not be reprimanded for doing so, no matter how annoying this violation of procedures may be. Any action on the part of management that could be interpreted as retaliation against a complainant should be carefully avoided.

While certain "management rights" such as the right to counsel, assign, transfer, discipline, evaluate, etc., may not be "grievable" under personnel rules or union contract terms, any management action is grievable if an element of discriminatory treatment is charged. Certain federal programs such as CETA may also have additional grievance mechanisms that apply even to probationary employees who under regular civil service or other rules would not be able to appeal discipline or termination before the end of the probationary period.

There are times when implementing affirmative action seems to consist of negative actions, such as I have just outlined. "Setting things right" is always difficult, and people resist basic behavior changes for a variety of reasons. It takes both energy and commitment over a long period of time to institute the changes in attitude and practice that are preconditions to real equal opportunity in any organization.

DEVELOPING AN AFFIRMATIVE ACTION PLAN

What can you do if your library does not have an affirmative action plan? It may be that the library administration does not realize that this is as much in violation of ALA policy as censorship of library materials is in violation of the Library Bill of Rights, which is also ALA policy. If your library receives as little as $2500 in federal funds and employs fifteen or more people, it may also be in violation of the law. Begin with a positive approach to management, pointing out the affirmative side of providing equal employment opportunity for all, with a gentle reminder of compliance as a side benefit. Offer to provide a list of readings and the fair employment laws, or to write a brief proposal to appoint a staff task force to develop a plan. If your library is involved in community analysis, you may have the opportunity to point out the need to hire employees who can relate to specific underserved groups, such as bilingual librarians to serve Hispanic users.

A written plan usually is prefaced by the policy statement which the plan is to implement. A typical policy might read:

> In accordance with existing Federal and State statutes and guidelines and in compliance with the Affirmative Action Program of the City of _____, it is and will continue to be the Policy of the _____ Public Library to provide equal opportunity to all applicants for employment and all employees, to administer all personnel practices such as recruitment, hiring, assignments, promotions, compensation, training, discipline and privileges of employment in a manner which does not discriminate on the basis of race, color, religion, ancestry, national origin, sex, age, disability, marital status, and sexual or affectional preference.
>
> This commitment is to be implemented through an Affirmative Action Program which will guide us to our goals in practical steps. This program includes guidelines to ensure proper treatment of each and every library applicant and employee, and of the users to whom we aspire to provide equal access to library and information services.
>
> Responsibility for implementing this policy is vested in the Office of the Library Director and in all management and supervisory personnel in the library, and was adopted by the Library Board as official policy on _____.

After the policy statement, the plan should delineate specific responsibilities of line management at all levels, and the role to be played by the staff advisory committee. An EEO coordinator should be named, responsible to the director, to serve as an auditor of personnel functions. There is some difference of opinion on whether the EEO officer should be separate from the personnel officer.[22] Problems or barriers to equal opportunity can be identified through written surveys or committee hearings. The first step is a utilization analysis, usually done in chart format, which will reveal quite clearly where employees are now clustered and where they are not utilized in the numbers they might reasonably have been if equal opportunity had existed in the past. The setting of voluntary goals (which are not the same as quotas set by the courts for failure to take affirmative action) most often occurs at the hiring level in recruiting minority librarians or male circulation clerks, but training and promotional goals may also be set. Once specific barriers have been identified and goals have been set, action programs are designed to reach the goals. I have already mentioned a few. Others could include: (1) career ladders to open paraprofessional positions to clerical workers, and to enable paraprofessionals to become librarians; (2) better dissemination of promotional opportunities in job openings and training programs; (3) regular and special orientation programs; (4) cultural awareness and human relations training for supervisors; (5) regular publication of affirmative action information in a library newsletter; (6) recruitment trips to library schools with minority students; (7) revision of discriminatory civil service or other personnel rules; (8) remodeling of work areas to remove architectural barriers for employees in wheelchairs or with other handicaps; and so on.

All of this should happen within a specific period of time and regular progress reports should be made to both management and staff. The plan should be updated regularly, preferably once a year, and it should be well-publicized among staff and in the community. An affirmative action plan can be a basic management tool to ensure that personnel policies are appropriately and consistently applied. If your library does not have a written personnel manual yet, an affirmative action plan can be the beginning. In fact, I believe that affirmative action has been the major catalyst prompting libraries to examine carefully all past personnel practices and to establish the written policies and procedures needed in so many libraries.

DEALING WITH REALITIES

So your library has adopted a written affirmative action plan and you have been conscientious in your commitment to the principles of equal opportunity in your daily work. What can you expect? First, expect your motives in establishing an affirmative action program to be suspect. If you are not seen as a "do-gooder" or "soft on minorities" (i.e., you treat some "more equally" than others), you will be seen as primarily interested in "covering your flank." Also, you should not expect gratitude from those benefiting from your programs, first, because they don't owe you anything, and second, because they are paying a price for the benefits they receive. It is not easy to be the first of anything in an organization, such as the first woman in a city department heads' meeting. The first minority librarian will see herself as only a token, because that is exactly what she is until there are many more like her, and she may tend to feel used in order "to make administration look good." Then there are those who will feel, no matter how careful and fair you try to be, that there is now less opportunity for them because they are not members of the protected classes.

A lot of hurt feelings and many confrontations may occur during the first years. Then, as the newly-hired grow and develop, promotional opportunities at the higher levels may not open as soon as necessary, and the library which has done a good job of recruiting and developing staff will lose them to other libraries with more sophisticated affirmative action programs and goals. Success requires much more than a written plan, no matter how often it is updated. It requires constant self-examination and self-criticism, willingness to admit mistakes and an ability to maintain transactions on an adult level in the face of the emotional situations and interpersonal stress that come with major organizational change. It requires constant verbal and written communication about your commitment to equal opportunity and what you are doing about it with both staff and the community. In the end, the emphasis is on action, with positive results in visible form.

It has been four years since E.J. Josey asked the question, "Can library affirmative action succeed?" Libraries still have a long way to go before we can answer in the affirmative. As he said then, "Higher education institutions and public libraries will not erase elitism or racism over night."[23] If this is to happen at all, it will require the positive efforts of all library trustees and higher education administrators, and of all library workers and librarians. It is not an easy task but I believe it is worth our energies. Ultimately, success in building a balanced and diversified staff will enable us to be much more responsive in meeting the library and information needs of the people we serve.

REFERENCES

1. Miniter, John J. "Implications of Affirmative Action in Recruitment, Employment and Termination of Personnel," *North Carolina Libraries* 36:16, Spring 1978.

2. Myers, Margaret, and Lynch, Beverly P. "Affirmative Action and Academic Libraries," *Directions* 1:13, Sept. 1975.

3. Ibid.

4. "Major Fair Employment Laws." *In* Robert Wedgeworth, ed. *ALA Yearbook: A Review of Library Events 1977.* Chicago, ALA, 1978, vol. 3, p. 224.

5. U.S. Equal Employment Opportunity Commission. *Affirmative Action and Equal Employment: A Guidebook for Employers.* 2 vols. Washington, D.C., U.S.E.E.O.C., Jan. 1974.

6. "ALA Equal Employment Subcommittee Guidelines for Library Affirmative Action Plans," *American Libraries* 7:451, July/Aug. 1976.

7. Dickinson, Elizabeth, and Myers, Margaret. "Affirmative Action and American Librarianship." *In* Michael H. Harris, ed. *Advances in Librarianship.* New York, Academic Press, 1978, vol. 8, pp. 81-133.

8. Rudy, Michelle. "Equity and Patterns of Library Governance," *Library Trends* 26:181-93, Fall 1977.

9. Maslow, Abraham H. *Eupsychian Management: A Journal* (Irwin-Dorsey Series in Behavioral Science). Homewood, Ill., Richard D. Irwin and Dorsey Press, 1965, p. 17.

10. The Fourteenth Amendment to the U.S. Constitution (1868) establishes the basis of U.S. citizenship and forbids states to abridge privileges of citizens or to deprive any person of life, liberty or property without due process of law, or to deny any person equal protection of the law.

11. Rudy, op. cit., pp. 190-91.

12. Myers and Lynch, op. cit., p. 15.

13. Clark, Grover M., and Perlman, Jeanette. "A New Approach to Affirmative Action Programs," *Supervisory Management* 22:14-15, Dec. 1977.

14. Ibid., pp. 11-12.

15. Genaway, David C. "Bar Coding and the Librarian Supermarket: An Analysis of Advertised Library Vacancies," *Library Journal* 103:325, Feb. 1, 1978.

16. Simon, Barry E. "To Ask or Not to Ask; Personnel Selection Practices: Applications and Interviews," *American Libraries* 9:141-43, March 1978.

17. "Race Bias Charge Nixed by N.Y. High Court," *Library Journal* 103:705-06, April 1, 1978.

18. Hall, Francine S. "Gaining EEO Compliance with a Stable Work Force," *Personnel Journal* 56:454, Sept. 1977.

19. Peres, Richard. *Dealing with Employment Discrimination.* New York, McGraw-Hill, 1978, p. 189.

20. Maslow, op. cit., p. 25.

21. Zerface, W.A. "Hire the Handicapped Librarian!" *Wilson Library Bulletin* 51:656-60, April 1977.

22. Anthony, William P., and Bowen, Marshall. "Affirmative Action: Problems and Promises," *Personnel Journal* 56:619, Dec. 1977.

23. Josey, E.J. "Can Library Affirmative Action Succeed?" *Library Journal* 100:31, Jan. 1, 1975.

CONTRIBUTORS

ELAINE M. ALBRIGHT is Executive Director of the Lincoln Trail Library System of central Illinois, a position she has held since 1977. Before that she was Associate Professor and Reference and Research Librarian at the University of Illinois at Urbana-Champaign, where she earned her master's degree in library science. She has served on numerous committees, both for the university and the state of Illinois, and has been active in various divisions of ALA and the Illinois Library Association.

HUGH C. ATKINSON is University Librarian and Professor of Library Administration at the University of Illinois at Urbana-Champaign. He received his MA at the Graduate Library School of the University of Chicago and has served in various capacities at college and university libraries across the country. He has been active in ALA since 1966 and is currently Vice-Chairperson of the Circulation Services Section of the Library Administration Division. He has written four books and over twenty articles.

MARTHA J. BAILEY is Assistant Professor and Physics Librarian of Purdue University. She graduated from Butler University in Indianapolis and received an MS in library science from Drexel University. She is a member of the Research Committee of ALA and has held offices in the Special Libraries Association and the American Society for Information Science. She has published six papers and one book on library management.

RICHARD CALABRESE is Associate Professor and Chairman of the Communication Arts and Sciences Department of Rosary College in River Forest, Illinois. He earned master's degrees in speech and theater, and English literature from Bradley University, and a Ph.D. in human communication from Northwestern University. He has written three scholarly articles and is responsible for the development of a Media Kit commissioned by the Illinois Library Association.

DAVID R. DOWELL is Assistant University Librarian for Personnel and Staff Development at Duke University. He received master's degrees in library science and Latin American history from the University of Illinois at Urbana-Champaign and is currently a doctoral student in library science at the University of North Carolina. He is an active member of ALA, the Association of College and Research Libraries and other professional organizations. He has delivered six addresses and written five articles for scholarly library journals.

AGNES M. GRIFFEN is Deputy Director of the Tucson Public Library. She earned a master's degree in librarianship from the University of Washington in Seattle, and served as Deputy Librarian and Coordinator of the King County Library System in that city. She is a member of ALA, the Arizona State Library Association and the Southwestern Library Association, and has published five articles on the subject of librarianship.

LARS LARSON is Associate Professor and former Associate Dean of the College of Business and Administration at Southern Illinois University at Carbondale. He received his MBA and Ph.D. from the University of Illinois at Urbana-Champaign, where he was Assistant Director of the Executive Development Center. He has served on the faculties of various administrative and organizational behavior programs, is a member of the Academy of Management, and a founder of Nova Associates, a management and administrative consulting group. He is coeditor of four books and author of several articles on leadership and motivation.

DONALD J. SAGER is Commissioner of the Chicago Public Library and former Director of the Public Library of Columbus and Franklin County in Columbus, Ohio, and the Kingston City Library in Kingston, New York. He received his MSLS from the University of Wisconsin at Madison. He is a member of ALA and the Ohio Library Association, where he has served as Chairman of the Audiovisual Services Round Table, the Staff Development Committee, and the Regional Reference Workshop Committee. He has written one book and contributed articles to scholarly publications.

ROLLAND E. STEVENS is Professor of Library Science at the University of Illinois at Urbana-Champaign, where he earned his MSLS and Ph.D. His previous positions include Bibliographer at the University of Illinois at Urbana-Champaign, and Associate Director of Technical Processes at Ohio State University Libraries. He is the author of *Reference Books in the Social Sciences and Humanities,* numerous articles and book reviews, and editor of several monographs and periodicals.

RICHARD J. VORWERK is Dean of Special Programs and Instructional Services at Governor's State University, Park Forest South, Illinois. His degrees include an MA in philosophy from Loyola University, and MA in library science and a Ph.D. in the administration of academic libraries, both from Indiana University. He is a member of several professional organizations, including ALA, the American Association of University Administrators, and the American Management Associations. He has coauthored one article and written book reviews for various journals.

ACRONYMS

AACR — Anglo-American Cataloging Rules
ALA — American Library Association
CETA — Comprehensive Employment and Training Act
EEO — Equal Employment Opportunity
GM — General Motors
LCS — Library Computer System
LPC — Least-Preferred Coworker
OCLC — Ohio College Library Center
OLPR — Office for Library Personnel Resources
OSHA — Occupational Safety and Health Administration

INDEX

Academic librarians. *See* Librarians, academic.

Affirmative action: necessity for, 94-96; impact of, on supervisory responsibilities, 96-97; and staff development, 98-99; and evaluation, 99-100; and adverse personnel actions, 100-03; and grievance procedures, 101-03.

Affirmative action plan, development of a, 104-05.

ALA/EEO policy, 94.

Annual reviews, 3. *See also* Evaluation.

Argyris, Chris, 52.

Authority, of supervisors, 34.

Automation, and effects on supervision, 6-7.

Bare, Alan, 57-58.

Barth's distinction, 9.

Binder, Michael B., 35-36.

Boyd, Bradford, 85.

Broadwell, Martin, 66.

Budgeting, and problems of service, 34.

Canelas, Dale B., 39.

Change, encouragement of, as motivator, 51.

Chemers, Martin M., 25.

Civil Rights Act of 1964, Title VII, 93.

Clark, Grover M., 97.

Clerical personnel. *See* Personnel, clerical.

Climate, Social. *See* Social climate.

Climate, Supportive. *See* Supportive climate.

Collective bargaining, 38.

Communication: and supervision, 75-79; upward, 76; nonverbal, 78-79; and discipline, 100-01.

Competence, and confusion with enthusiasm, 4.

Conflict, among workers, 77.

Continuing education: 60-61; and staff development, difference between, 62.

Decision-making: 16-17; participative, 52.

Decision process, flowchart of, 18.

Dickinson, Elizabeth, 94.

Directives, enforcement of, 35.

Disciplinary action, 87-88.

Discipline: and proper documentation, 100-01; and communication, 100-01; and evaluation, 100-01.

Dowling, William F., 88.

Drucker, Peter, 45.

Education, Continuing. *See* Continuing education.

EEO: 38; violations of, 41; regulations of, and duplication of federal, state and local laws, 93-94; and ALA/EEO policy, 94.

Effectiveness, of leaders, 11.

Enthusiasm, and confusion with competence, 4.

Equal Opportunity Act of 1972, 93.

Evaluation: of output, 2; quality and quantity of, 2; and need for documentation, 2; problems with, 3-4; and importance of interview with person evaluated, 5; and testimony of those served, 5; and affirmative action, 99-100. *See also* Annual reviews.

Faculty status, of academic librarians, 36.

Fiedler, Fred E., 24, 25, 26.

Flex-time, 36-37.

Fry, Bernard M., 30.

Gamaluddin, Ahmad F., 36.

Genaway, David, 97.

Grievance procedures, 101-03.